HOW TO GIVE
EFFECTIVE
BUSINESS
BRIEFINGS

HOW TO GIVE EFFECTIVE BUSINESS BRIEFINGS

EFFECTIVE TECHNIQUES FOR RELAYING INFORMATION TO AND OBTAINING FEEDBACK FROM EMPLOYEES

COLIN CLARK

KOGAN PAGE
BETTER MANAGEMENT SKILLS

YOURS TO HAVE AND TO HOLD

BUT NOT TO COPY

First published in 1999

Kogan Page Limited
120 Pentonville Road
London N1 9JN

British Library Cataloguing in Publication Data

A CIP record for this book is available from the British Library.

ISBN 0 7494 2513 X

Typeset by Kogan Page
Printed and bound by Clays Ltd, St Ives plc

Contents

Contents

Preface

Eighty-two per cent of the 915 UK organizations surveyed by the Industrial Society in 1994 used briefings to relay information to and obtain feedback from their employees. Briefings were not only one of the most common ways of communicating between managers and staff teams, they were also seen as being, by far, the most effective.

Today, such business briefings are conducted by almost every kind of manager, supervisor and leader in almost every kind of organization. When they are held regularly and delivered effectively they can have a dramatic influence on employee performance, the quality of management–staff relationships and, more generally, on the success of the organization itself.

This book aims to provide you with the information you need to prepare and deliver high quality business briefings. The following chapters contain a mixture of advice, examples, exercises, checklists and short tests based on best practice from real-life business briefings. Together, they will help you relay your information to and obtain valuable feedback from the people you brief, in a more efficient and effective way.

The many benefits of business briefings cannot, of course, be guaranteed. But with this book, and a commitment from you to conduct business briefings regularly and effectively, these benefits will undoubtedly be much easier to achieve.

Colin Clark

CHAPTER 1
Introduction

Before you can brief people effectively it is important to appreciate exactly what business briefings are, what they can achieve and what factors determine their ultimate success.

Typically, business briefings are:

- short (eg 15–30 minutes);
- face-to-face meetings;
- conducted by managers, supervisors, work-group leaders, etc;
- on a regular basis (eg monthly, weekly, daily);
- given to groups of people employed in the same organization;
- given to those personnel who share the same status or work on the same kinds of tasks;
- held to relay information to and/or obtain information from the people being briefed;
- held in order to initiate some particular action and/or achieve some specific objective.

Business briefings can be an upward, horizontal or downward communication process to superiors, equals or subordinates. They are, however, most often given to small, team-sized groups of employees by their immediate and familiar superior. This is why, in this book, I have concentrated primarily on the skills you will need for 'downward' briefing of your own staff. Chapter 11 contains advice on the other types of briefings you are likely to encounter or deliver in your organization.

Business briefings are an ideal forum for the following kinds of activities:

- *Informing*. Relaying messages to others within an organization to enhance the understanding of the people being briefed.
- *Deciding*. Reviewing, debating or evaluating the merits of an issue or to reach a decision, perhaps from a number of alternatives.
- *Developing*. Giving advice, recognition, support or encouragement to others to maintain or improve their level of commitment, effort or performance.
- *Discussing*. Raising relevant issues or activities in order to obtain information or feedback from the people being briefed, to solve a problem or to steer people in a particular direction.
- *Activating*. Announcing and allocating particular work tasks among the people being briefed to achieve specific targets and objectives.

The recent and rapid growth in the popularity of business briefings is not just the result of many organizations adopting a more open and consultative management style; in today's world such briefings are a necessity. Modern organizations need to make informed decisions, to relay information to, and obtain feedback from, their employees and to put into action various strategies and plans at a speed rarely experienced by previous generations. More decisions have to be made and more information has to be processed, relayed and acted on, yet less time is available to do this before an opportunity is lost or a potential advantage missed. Business briefings are proving to be a highly successful way of dealing with these kinds of problems, but are not just a particular kind of meeting held for a particular kind of purpose. They are also the result of a particular kind of commitment – a commitment to inform, involve and consult others within an organization. The success of business briefings depends crucially on a series of ongoing commitments that you, the people you brief and your organization all need to make to one another. The types of commitments that need to be made are:

- to champion the importance and the advantages of having a genuinely two-way flow of open, high quality and informative communication between all employees and at all levels of your organization;
- to ensure that all employees are highly trained in communication skills. Briefers need this form of training to relay their information effectively. The recipients of briefings need it to successfully act on

the information they receive and to feed back their opinions and experiences to their briefers;
- to ensure that briefers consult with, listen to and act on the feedback they obtain from their briefings;
- to ensure that recipients of briefings will listen to and act on the information they are given and be provided with adequate training, time, resources and support to do so.

The Reality of Organizations' Commitment to Employee Communication?
An Industrial Society survey of 915 UK organizations found that nearly three quarters of employers had no written policy on employee communications. Three quarters of employers had no specific budget for employee communications. Just over half of these organizations had someone who was specifically responsible for employee communications. One in four organizations made no attempt to measure the effectiveness of their employee communications and only one in ten actually costed the time spent on this activity.

Source: Managing Best Practice: (Report no. 1) *Employee Communications*. London: The Industrial Society. May 1994.

What briefings can and cannot achieve

Effective business briefings can generate important benefits for you, the people you brief and your organization more generally. These benefits include:

- *Increased performance.* People will be more able to work to their full potential and accomplish their tasks and targets with a greater level of consistency and certainty.
- *Higher morale.* Team-spirit, motivation, enthusiasm and a sense of involvement in the organization will be heightened.
- *Greater understanding.* Employers, managers and staff will have a better knowledge of what is happening in their organization and why, as well as what their particular tasks and responsibilities are.

- *Enhanced relationships*. Different levels of the organization's hierarchy will be better equipped to listen to, co-operate with and appreciate the importance of each other's roles and points of view.
- *Improved efficiency*. Employees at different levels of the organization's hierarchy will be more able to quickly communicate with and respond to one another's needs, problems and objectives.

To obtain these benefits, business briefings *must* be conducted regularly and effectively by highly skilled managers, supervisors, work-group leaders, etc. Everyone in the organization also has to be both fully committed to and able to make the most of open and high quality communication. Business briefings, on their own, can never remedy the problems created by bad or non-existent training, inadequate resources, low wages or poor working conditions, etc – no matter how effectively they are delivered.

Your answers to the following questions will give you a basic idea of the level of commitment your organization has made towards having effective internal communication.

	Yes	No	Don't know
1. Your organization is open, flexible and consultative between and within all levels of its hierarchy.	___	___	___
2. You have received high quality training in briefing skills.	___	___	___
3. The feedback you obtain from your briefings is regularly listened to and acted on by your superiors.	___	___	___
4. Your organization has a formal, written policy on employee communications.	___	___	___
5. Your organization has a specific budget for employee communications.	___	___	___

	Yes	No	Don't know
6. There is someone who is specifically responsible for employee communications in your organization.	____	____	____
7. The people you brief are given sufficient training, time resources and support to complete their tasks and achieve targets and objectives.	____	____	____
8. The quality and effectiveness of your briefings are monitored regularly by higher management.	____	____	____
9. You can provide a recent example where information that was relayed up to senior management resulted in a change in policy or strategy within your organization.	____	____	____

The more you answer 'no' or 'don't know' to these questions the greater is the likelihood that the effectiveness of your business briefings will be compromised by an attitude within your organization that does not appreciate the importance of open and effective internal communication. Even if such an attitude does not exist within your organization, for you, the difficulty and the responsibility of being an effective business briefer will always remain.

CHAPTER 2
Background

Effective business briefers have five common qualities:

1. *A high level of communication skill.* They are able to successfully relay information to and obtain information from others. The people they brief regularly appreciate and act on the information they are given and consistently achieve their set targets and objectives.
2. *A high level of commitment.* They continually strive to improve their own communication and management skills and to facilitate improvements in the skills of the people they brief.
3. *A high level of awareness.* They recognize the often subtle communication tactics and strategies that are needed to deliver successful briefings.
4. *A positive attitude.* They are optimists who have confidence in and respect the abilities and opinions of the people they brief. They are also aware of the need to be open, flexible and consultative during a briefing.
5. *A positive approach.* They are realistic and pragmatic and put their positive attitude into action during their business briefings.

The following test measures the quality of your *current* briefing attitudes and skills in each of these five key areas. It will help you discover which skills you may need to improve and which attitudes you may have to change to become a better business briefer. Rate yourself (ranging from 'never' to 'always') for each of the statements below depending on how frequently each particular statement applies to you. Answer each statement in terms of how you actually think, feel or behave *now*. Be as honest and accurate as you can.

1. Communication skills

	Never	Seldom		Sometimes	Often	Always

	Never	Seldom		Sometimes		Often	Always
1. During my briefings I receive many positive acknowledgements (such as 'Yeah', 'Right', 'Mm hmm') from the people I brief.	0	1	2	3	4	5
2. The people I brief understand every important point I make.	0	1	2	3	4	5
3. I am able, when necessary, to persuade the people I brief to change their opinions and behaviour.	0	1	2	3	4	5
4. I give reasons and explanations for all the important things I ask the people I brief to do.	0	1	2	3	4	5
5. I receive lots of constructive feedback from the people I brief.	0	1	2	3	4	5
6. The people I brief satisfactorily complete their tasks and achieve the targets I set.	0	1	2	3	4	5
7. The people I brief use the advice I give them.	0	1	2	3	4	5
8. I have to work hard to keep the people I brief interested in what I am saying.	5	4	3	2	1	0
9. There are one or two cliques in the people I brief.	5	4	3	2	1	0
10. I have to keep repeating advice and instructions to the people I brief.	5	4	3	2	1	0

Mark your total on the scale below.

Communication skills

Low										High
0	5	10	15	20	25	30	35	40	45	50

2. Level of commitment

	Never	Seldom		Sometimes	Often	Always
11. I take special steps to make each briefing better than the last.	0	1	2	3	4	5
12. I read books and articles to improve my skills as a manager, communicator and briefer.	0	1	2	3	4	5
13. Successful briefings are a collaborative process where the contributions of briefer and briefed are equally important.	0	1	2	3	4	5
14. I evaluate the impact my briefings have on the people I brief.	0	1	2	3	4	5
15. I work from the assumption that every deficiency in the subsequent performance of the people I brief is a result of a deficiency in my own briefing and management ability.	0	1	2	3	4	5
16. I informally ask the people I brief about the effectiveness of the advice I give them.	0	1	2	3	4	5
17. I take special steps to obtain feedback from the people I brief.	0	1	2	3	4	5

18. I lead by example; I am not too proud to pitch in with the people I brief or help them achieve the objectives I set.　　0　　1　　2　　3　　4　　5

19. Effective communication depends on natural ability not hard work or learned skills.　　5　　4　　3　　2　　1　　0

20. I discourage the people I brief from consulting with and advising each other.　　5　　4　　3　　2　　1　　0

Mark your total on the scale below.

Level of commitment

Low										High
0	5	10	15	20	25	30	35	40	45	50

---

3. Level of awareness

	Never	Seldom	Sometimes		Often	Always

21. The people I brief need accurate information and useful advice, not empty motivational 'rah-rah' phrases.　　0　　1　　2　　3　　4　　5

22. I continually monitor the people I brief for changes in their level of interest and involvement.　　0　　1　　2　　3　　4　　5

23. When the people I brief stay silent it means that some form of 'trouble' is on its way.　　0　　1　　2　　3　　4　　5

24. I listen for hints in the comments and feedback from the people I brief. Such implicit talk may indicate what they may be really thinking or feeling.　　0　　1　　2　　3　　4　　5

25. Prevention is better than cure.	0	1	2	3	4	5
26. I deliberately try to make each of my briefings different.	0	1	2	3	4	5
27. Real-life body-language, on its own, is easy to interpret accurately.	5	4	3	2	1	0
28. Criticism is a better motivator than praise.	5	4	3	2	1	0
29. Most people are more or less the same and can be treated as such.	5	4	3	2	1	0
30. Empowered people are more likely to be ineffective people.	5	4	3	2	1	0

Mark your total on the scale below.

Level of awareness

Low										High
0	5	10	15	20	25	30	35	40	45	50

4. Attitude

	Never	Seldom	Sometimes	Often	Always
31. The subsequent performance of the people I brief is the best benchmark of my ability as a briefer.	0	1	2	3	4	5
32. I have confidence in the abilities of the people I brief.	0	1	2	3	4	5
33. If I do not control the people I brief they will end up controlling me.	5	4	3	2	1	0
34. Giving a concession to the people I brief is a sign of weakness.	5	4	3	2	1	0

35. Briefings are best held only
if and when they are necessary.   5   4   3   2   1   0

36. If I had better people to
work with I would be a better
manager/briefer.   5   4   3   2   1   0

37. To be a successful briefer
you have to keep your distance
from the people you brief.   5   4   3   2   1   0

38. Nobody who receives a
decent salary should ever need
motivating.   5   4   3   2   1   0

39. The people I brief moan and
groan about the smallest things.   5   4   3   2   1   0

40. If I am honest, I take
personal criticism personally.   5   4   3   2   1   0

Mark your total on the scale below.

Attitude
Negative   **Positive**
0   5   10   15   20   25   30   35   40   45   50

---

5. Approach

| | Seldom | | Often | |
Never		Sometimes		Always

41. I encourage the people I
brief to express different ideas
and opinions to my own.

0   1   2   3   4   5

42. I will change my point of
view if someone proposes a
solution to a problem that is
better than my own.   0   1   2   3   4   5

43. I show the people I brief that I do not hold a grudge if they constructively criticize the things I say or ask them to do.	0	1	2	3	4	5
44. I 'pull rank' over the people I brief (eg by saying 'You *will* do X because *I* say so'.)	5	4	3	2	1	0
45. Rightly or wrongly, I get angry at the people I brief when they perform much worse than I expected.	5	4	3	2	1	0
46. Fear (such as the threat of dismissal) can be an extremely powerful motivator of the people I brief.	5	4	3	2	1	0
47. During my briefings I tend to dwell on the negative rather than the positive aspects of the performance of the people I brief.	5	4	3	2	1	0
48. I interrupt the people I brief as soon as I have understood the thrust of what they are saying.	5	4	3	2	1	0
49. My briefings are a serious business and that is why I avoid using humour.	5	4	3	2	1	0
50. I only give information to the people I brief on a 'need to know' basis.	5	4	3	2	1	0

Mark your total on the scale below.

Approach

Negative										Positive
0	5	10	15	20	25	30	35	40	45	50

Now check your score:

If you scored 35 or over in *all five key areas*: you already are an accomplished business briefer. If you are certain that your answers reflect your actual briefing attitudes and behaviour then this book will help you maintain your already high level of aptitude and skill.

If you scored between 20–34 in *a key area*: with a little more effort and fine tuning you should be able to make significant improvements in this important aspect of your briefing ability.

If you scored 19 or under in *a key area*: you will probably benefit from revising your current attitudes or behaviour in this key area. With the help of this book and a willingness to improve you could make dramatic progress as a business briefer.

Study each of these 50 statements again. Make a note of which particular skills and attitudes you ought to improve.

- Which of the five key areas are you strongest in?
- Which key area are you weakest in and need to concentrate on the most?

Effective business briefing begins with a combination of:

PROPER PREPARATION

of

INFORMATION

that is

SUCCESSFULLY DELIVERED

within a briefing that has both

STRUCTURE

and

IMPACT

These topics are examined in greater detail in Chapters 3 to 6. You should read these chapters together to obtain the best possible benefits from them.

CHAPTER 3
Preparation

The key to delivering an effective business briefing is proper preparation. However, the urgency with which information all too often has to be relayed to people in modern organizations means you will rarely have enough time to plan your briefings properly and few opportunities to rehearse what you intend to say. This chapter shows you how to make the most of the time you have available to assemble and organize an effective briefing plan.

> Most of the briefings I've given have had to be last minute, impromptu affairs. Looking back, I'm certain I'd have been far more successful not only if I'd had more time to prepare but also if I'd known how to use what little time I had available in the best possible way.
>
> **Sales manager**

All business briefings should be objective driven. Ideally, they should also have a single objective. An objective is your aim or intention, the outcome you desire or require from the subject-matter of your briefing. Some typical examples are given on page 15.

Everything you say in your briefing should be geared toward promoting and achieving an objective. For many managers, particularly those giving downward briefings, much of the subject matter of your briefings will already be defined, at least in general terms, by information more senior personnel require you to deliver to the people you brief. In every case, however, your first task will be to prepare the actual content of your briefing. The following three-step question-answer strategy will help you do this.

Type of Briefing	Subject Matter	Objective
Information	Report how the recent take-over will result in a restructuring of our company.	To successfully increase understanding.
Decision	Evaluate which departments should receive the remaining funds in the training budget.	To reach the decision.
Development	Instruct the staff how to lay the dining tables for the evening banquet.	To provide effective practical assistance.
Discussion	Discover exactly what the engineers need to do to reduce the recent spate of production line stoppages.	To obtain sufficient feedback to solve the problem.
Action	Sell 15% per cent more mobile telephones over the next four weeks.	To accomplish the task.

Step 1. Basics

You first have to be very clear about exactly what information you need to relay or obtain. Then (and *only* then) you should ask yourself the following questions:

- **What** is my objective?
- **How** can this objective be achieved?
- **Why** does this objective need to be achieved?
- **Where** will the tasks needed to accomplish this objective be carried out?
- **Who** will be responsible for doing which particular tasks?

- **When** will these tasks be attempted and over what time period do they have to be achieved?

Write down *very specific* answers to all these questions. The more specific you are the more effective your preparation and your subsequent briefing is likely to be. The notes you make here will form the basic substance of your briefing.

Step 2. Environment

You will need to determine what factors, both within and outside of your organization, may adversely influence the attitudes, behaviour and performance of the people you brief and, as such, the chances of achieving your objective. Examples of negative *internal* factors are:

- Poor or non-existent training of both briefers and briefed.
- Demotivated staff.
- Inadequate resources.
- Insufficient time.
- Lack of personal support of both briefers and briefed.

Examples of negative *external* factors are:

- Customer reluctance to buy what you are offering for sale.
- Poor weather or road/transport conditions.
- Unpredictable exchange rate fluctuations.
- Inconsistent supply or delivery of raw materials or stock.

Write any such negative factors down and then ask yourself if the people you are going to brief have:

- the **knowledge**;
- the **resources**;
- the **ability**;
- the **time**;
- the **support**;
- and the **motivation**

. . . to perform to the best of their ability and accomplish the objective of your briefing?

If you answer no to any of these questions you will almost certainly need to prepare additional information, resources, advice, support and training to help the people you brief to overcome these factors before your objective can be achieved.

More generally, gear the content of your briefing towards the people you are going to brief. Ask yourself: 'What are the negatives people will be thinking when I relay my information to them?' 'How are they likely to react to what I am are proposing they should do?' Incorporate into your briefing preparation answers to the problems they are likely to face and the reservations and objections they are likely to express.

Step 3. Degree of objective difficulty

Objectives differ in terms of the degree of control that you and the people you brief have over the types of internal and external factors mentioned above. Some objectives are relatively simple and have highly predictable and controllable results. In these cases your briefing will need little more than basic information in the form of instructions, explanations and practical advice.

Other objectives are more complex and have more unpredictable and uncontrollable outcomes. In these cases you may need to do *additional* work to encourage and motivate the people you brief. The greater the degree of influence of external factors on the outcome of your objective the more unpredictable and uncontrollable that outcome is likely to be.

Support

To help you answer the questions in each of the three steps above and to provide high quality support for your briefing you should gather material in the form of facts, opinions, experiences and illustrations. The most popular ways of doing this are by:

- using feedback from previous briefings with the people you are about to brief;
- consulting other people for their opinions and experiences of the subject matter of your briefing;
- observation;
- reading relevant material from inside and outside your organization;
- personal experience.

The briefing planner

The following template will help you rapidly organize the notes you make.

Date: ..../..../.....	Briefer:		Page:
OBJECTIVE	....		
	ORDER		
TASK(S)	....	....	
INFORMATION & ADVICE **WHO WHAT WHERE WHEN WHY HOW**	....	....	
OTHER COMMENTS **(eg INTERNAL & EXTERNAL FACTORS)**	....	....	

Figure 1 *Briefing planner template*

Although what you write on this template should always be as specific and detailed as possible, you should not get into the habit of writing out verbatim everything you intend to say. Key words, figures and brief phrases will suffice. Write your points down in any order during your preparation. You can then use the second column of this template to order your points in the sequence you intend to deliver them.

Multi-objective briefings

In reality, your briefings will often consist of a number of objectives and contain a range of tasks and targets to specify and allocate, along with various other bits and pieces of unrelated information that needs to be said or obtained. Indeed, many business briefings consist of a combination of information, decision, development, discussion and action components.

In multi-objective briefings you should use a separate briefing planner template for each major objective or topic of your briefing. You will also have to order and prioritize what you are going to say. Psychologists have found that it is usually pointless to mention more than seven different items of information in an oral presentation as this is usually the maximum a listener is likely to remember. If you have many more than seven major topics or points to make then try to decide which of these can be omitted and relayed by some other means (eg via a memo or e-mail, etc) or presented, instead, at another briefing.

Topic position and topic content

List all your objectives, topics and points. Then rate them in an order of priority. You can prioritize by:

- **importance:** eg what needs saying or doing first?
- **logic or chronological sequence:** eg which particular task has to be completed or which particular procedure has to be explained before another can be mentioned?
- **interest:** eg what topic will people be most keen to hear about?

It is often best to place your most important, immediately relevant or interesting topic first. Bear in mind that information delivered at the beginning or end of a briefing is generally remembered more. Similarly, information delivered in the first half of a briefing tends to be remembered more than information delivered in the second half. Furthermore, if the points you intend to make are equally important then don't place those which are harder to understand in the middle of your briefing. This is where the attention of the people you brief is most likely to wander and where what you say is least likely to be remembered.

Select the order of each major objective, topic or point and staple the Briefing Planner templates together. You have now prepared your briefing plan.

Arranging your briefing

The people who should attend your briefing are those who need to know what you have to say and/or have the information you need to obtain. Having decided who these people are you should also consider the advantage of inviting anyone else who, although they may not be directly involved in the subject of your briefing, would nevertheless benefit from being present and consulted.

Give everyone plenty notice of where and when your briefing will take place. If necessary, provide people with details of how to get to the chosen location. You may also need to:

- confirm attendance;
- circulate any information that needs to be read before the briefing;
- ask people to be ready to provide feedback on certain issues, points or problems that will be raised.

Location
Try to hold your briefing where you will not be disrupted and where any potential distractions can be reduced to an absolute minimum. Be aware that noise can be distracting even when it does not obviously interrupt what you are saying or turn the heads of the people you are briefing.

Should everyone be seated or standing for your briefing? In the briefings I have conducted, attended or studied there seems to be an added sense of purpose and importance if everyone stands. At the very least it encourages brevity because your legs will invariably start to ache long before your jaw begins to tire. The exceptions to this advice are when you expect your briefing to be very long or if the people you brief will need to take many notes. However, you should be seated if they are seated; if they are standing then you too should stand.

Duration

Many business briefings last between 15 to 30 minutes. However, there is only one rule about how long a briefing ought to last: not a moment longer than it needs to be. Your briefing should not be so short that you cannot convey or obtain information in the detail required; and it should not be so long that you give people too much information to digest or you otherwise tax their patience. Briefings, therefore, do not actually have to be brief, only concise and purposeful. Of course, the actual length of your briefings are going to vary depending on how regularly they are conducted and what needs to be said within them. But, above all, ensure that it is the quality of what you say and not simply the quantity that determines how long your briefing lasts.

My advice for anyone wanting to know how long briefings should be? It's simple! Aim to finish talking before they finish listening. How many of us *always* do that?

Hotel Manager

If the time you have available for briefing is limited or restricted in some way this will obviously affect the amount of information you will be able to relay or obtain. Under these circumstances, while you prepare your briefing you should also prioritize your information into 'essential', 'important' and 'useful' categories. Progressively remove information from the latter categories until your time-slot has been filled.

Be strict about the start and finish time of your briefings. It is good practice to always allow for the possibility that your briefing might run over the allotted time as a result of your having to deal with any extra (particularly unexpected) feedback you may receive.

As you gain experience in preparing your briefings the preparation strategies outlined in this chapter will become second nature to you. You are also likely to find that the time you need to spend preparing will decline whilst the quality of what you prepare is maintained or even improves.

How to Give Effective Business Briefings

The following checklist will help you determine which aspects of your briefing preparation you need to improve.

	Always	Often / Occasionally		Rarely	Never
1. I do not have enough time to prepare properly.	5	4	3	2	1
2. I find it hard to identify the objective(s) of my briefing.	5	4	3	2	1
3. I find it difficult to decide what to include and what to leave out of my briefings.	5	4	3	2	1
4. I have problems in prioritizing my objectives, topics or points.	5	4	3	2	1
5. I forget to mention one or more key points.	5	4	3	2	1
6. I receive questions and feedback that I had not expected.	5	4	3	2	1

If you scored higher than 6: the quality of your briefings is likely to be suffering because of a lack of proper preparation. If you scored between 7–12: your lack of preparation will typically have a *low* influence on your ability to deliver your briefings effectively. If you scored between 13–18: your lack of preparation will typically have a *medium* influence on your ability to deliver your briefings effectively. If you scored 19 or over: your lack of preparation will typically have a *high* influence on your ability to deliver your briefings effectively. The higher your score, the more urgent it is that you take steps to improve your preparation.

CHAPTER 4
Structure

Information that is communicated in an organized way will have a higher impact on the people you brief simply because it will be much easier for them to follow, remember and act on. This chapter shows you how to structure your business briefing as a whole as well as each individual topic within it.

> Everybody knows the old saying about how you're supposed to deliver a speech – *any* speech: 'First, you tell people what you're going to say, then you say it, and then you tell them what you've just said'. And so you should. But, in my experience, a good structure is rarely as simple as that. To be really effective you need to do a lot more than that. A *whole lot more*, in fact.
> **Management Trainer**

As the quote above suggests, briefings should have an obvious beginning, middle and end taking the form of, respectively, an introduction, the various topics and points of your briefing, and a summary reiterating and reviewing what you have said. However, as we shall see, this basic layout is the absolute minimum you need to do.

The introduction

An effective introduction consists of a short outline of the main content and objective of your briefing. The following example contains all five of the key ingredients of an effective introduction:

'Good morning everyone. We need to regain the market share we lost in our last financial quarter. So today I'll be concentrating on the three ways we can improve our business performance by ten per cent between May and December. *First*, by establishing a completely new prospect territory. *Second*, by increasing our sales of higher margin stock. And, *third*, by visiting our existing customers more often.'

- It is **short and succinct**. (It took only around 25 seconds for this manager to deliver, and no point took longer than a sentence to express.)
- It mentions the **objective(s)** of the briefing. (ie To 'regain lost market share' and to 'improve business performance by ten per cent'.)
- It lists the main **topics** (or points) of the briefing (ie 'First' . . .; 'Second' . . .; 'Third' . . .)
- It indicates the **ways and means** by which the objective(s) can be achieved (eg 'by establishing a completely new prospect territory'.)
- It specifies, where appropriate, a **time scale** within which the objective is to be achieved. (ie 'between May and December'.)

You do not have to trouble people with anything too elaborate or detailed at this stage. Specific facts and fine print are best left for the substance phase of your briefing. A single sentence for the 'What?', 'How?', 'Where?' and 'When?' elements of your briefing is often all you need to properly prepare everyone for what is coming. If you have a multi-objective briefing try to think of a general theme to announce in your introduction that links together all your objectives into a single, common and overall objective. If you have a list of points then telegraph the number of points you are going to make (eg 'I've got *five* points to mention. *First*, . . .', etc).

As well as outlining the content of your briefing, an introduction also sets its tone. Treat it, therefore, as an opportunity to positively influence the mood of your listeners. Be upbeat. Avoid sounding negative, hesitant, critical or defeatist. If you have to raise a problem try to ensure that your introduction focuses less on the problem itself than on how you are going to propose it can be solved.

The summary

Your summary is one of the most important parts of your briefing. The last thing people listen to is often the thing they remember most. Yet summaries can also be one of the most difficult parts of a briefing to deliver successfully. If you have delivered a poor briefing, a straight recap of what you have just said is probably the last thing your listeners will want to hear. Indeed, the lowest point of audience attention during a briefing is often at the point when you announce the start of your summary and thus telegraph the end of your briefing (eg by saying something like: 'In conclusion'; 'Finally'; 'To sum up'; 'Last of all'). At this point you may have to take special steps to ensure that everyone continues to listen to your summary. Here is one example of what you can do:

> '*Right*, put your pens in your pockets and *look at me please.*'
> [Pause]
> '*Just for one moment.*'
> [Pause]
> '*So*, to *summarize:*'
> [Pause]
> '*First*, we'll establish the completely new prospect territory by . . . '

This sequence contains three techniques to help keep everyone listening a little longer to what you still have to say:

1. An attention grabbing phrase (ie '*Right*', '*look at me please*').
2. Short pauses at each step to establish brief eye contact with your audience and to check they are paying attention.
3. An incentive to keep listening, such as a reference to the brevity of the time you are going to need before completing your summary (ie '*Just for one moment*').

Whatever you want people to do, wherever else you have told them and whatever has been decided or agreed upon, make sure you mention it again in your summary.

- Summaries, like introductions, are not the place for detail. Ensure you put more emphasis on the 'What?', the 'Where?' and the 'When?' elements of your briefing, rather than on the 'How?' and the 'Why?' elements.
- A summary should restate (but not slavishly repeat) only your most important points.
- Do not dilute the power of your summary by adding any new information.

- Keep things simple and easy to follow. (You can do this by making the order of the points in your summary the same as in the substance phase of your briefing.)
- The task/objective section of each Briefing Planner Template (see Chapter 2) can be used as 'point prompters' when delivering your end of briefing summary.

Structuring individual topics

Briefings that have an obvious beginning and end can be structured even further by explicitly marking the start and finish of each topic you raise. In this way you create a clear distinction between different items of information in the substance phase of your brief and make what you say much easier for people to follow. The following six steps will help you do this:

1. **Pause** for a short moment (ie a second or so) between the end of one topic and the beginning of the next to punctuate the two topics.
2. **Mark** your new topic with either a 'transitional' word (eg 'Right', 'Next') or, better still, a number ('First', 'Second', 'Third', etc) to affirm the completion of your previous topic.
3. **Emphasize** the first word or phrase of your new topic by speaking in a louder voice.
4. **Headline** each new topic with a short, easy to understand, single sentence announcement of the subject of your next topic.
5. **Pause** again after announcing your headline phrase.
6. **Begin** the first point of your new topic.

This is not as over-elaborate or time consuming as it first appears. The manager in the following sequence took less than ten seconds to move smoothly and informally through all six of the steps mentioned above:

'. . . so, thanks to all those people who stayed behind last night to help with planning our new sales territory.'
(1) [Pause.]
(2 & 3) '*Moving on*. Point number *two*.
(4) How to sell more higher margin stock:'
(5) [Pause.]
(6) 'Our sales of higher margin stock for the last quarter was much lower than it should have been ...'

Again, you should use each pause to quickly establish eye contact with your audience and to check that everyone is paying attention before you continue.

Structuring the entry and exit points of your topics will improve the attention, interest and concentration of the people you brief. By doing this you also provide anyone whose attention has wandered with an obvious opportunity point to rejoin your briefing before you begin a next topic.

Headlines

The advertising guru David Ogilvy claimed that only five per cent of the readers of print advertisements read beyond a headline. He concluded that headlines that do not inform people of the product on offer or tempt people to read further are liable, therefore, to lose 95 per cent of their potential readership. Much the same can be said about topic headlines in business briefings. As Figure 2 on page 28 shows, although the level of interest and attention of the people you are briefing is likely to be high when you announce a new topic, this may only be temporary. A problem you are likely to face at these points – a problem which often gets progressively worse the longer your briefing lasts – is that of sustaining this level of interest and attention for the duration of your upcoming topic. So, unless your headline sells what you are going to say, and unless you can convince people it will be worth their while to pay attention to you for longer than your headline, you may lose your listeners before you even begin your next topic.

Topic headlines should quickly and succinctly inform people about the general subject matter of your next topic. Basic headlines include:

- 'How to sell higher margin stock.'
- 'Important lesson about customer service today.'
- 'Very useful news about our product guarantees.'

Headlines are not the place for a complex sentence or a long-winded speech:

- 'The next topic is about the various ways in which you'll all be able to make improvements to your ability to sell more of the higher margin stock that's being lying in the basement for the last three and a half months . . .'

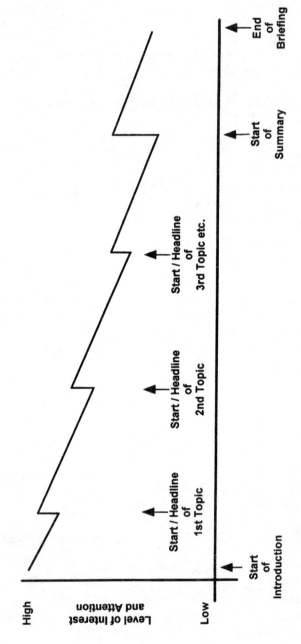

Figure 2 *Variations in levels of audience interest and attention during a typical business briefing*

. . . or any kind of vagueness:

- 'Here's something else for you.'
- 'Just a couple of things to say today.'
- 'Another point worth mentioning.'

Like introductions, headlines set the tone for what follows, so be positive:

- Use confident and commanding headlines. Avoid words like 'How we *may, (might, can, could possibly)* achieve X.' Replace them with words which convey a high degree of certainty and conviction like 'How we *can, (will, are going to,* etc) achieve X'.
- Telegraph a benefit in your headline (eg some information that will help the people you brief perform more effectively).
- Phrase your headlines as solutions, not problems; as answers, not questions.

If you find it difficult to invent a headline, try the following three-step strategy:

1. Ask yourself what word or short phrase sums up the **main point** of your topic?
2. Ask yourself what word or short phrase sums up the **desired outcome** of your topic.
3. Add the two together and you have the makings of a basic **headline**.

Effective headlines not only inform people of your upcoming topic, they also grab their attention. Words such as 'new', 'free', 'easier', 'improvement', 'time-saving', 'more effective', 'better' are ideal for this purpose.

To boost interest and memorability even further, use snappy sentences which capture the essence of your topic in a dramatic, highly unusual or even humorous way. This effect was achieved in a study of the British police force where station officers were instructed to employ such 'memory-trigger' phrases during briefings to their police colleagues. One officer used the phrase: 'Flasher in Full Bloom' to showcase a suspect wearing flower patterned underpants who had recently been seen indecently exposing himself. In another case, a search for a doorstep milk thief was announced with the headline:

'Pinta Pincher'. Try, though, to avoid being too gimmicky when you do this.

Think of your structure as the backbone of your business briefing: It is impossible to function effectively without it; it holds everything in its proper place; it's obviously there, even though it's hidden from view, but it's never so obvious that it draws attention to itself. Sectioning your information into chunks with clear beginnings and endings will enable you to deliver a briefing which fits together into a tight, coherent whole that progresses naturally and effortlessly from start to finish.

Structure checklist

Rate the following six key areas of briefing structure in terms of what you need to concentrate on most to improve the structure of your own business briefings. (1 = most improvement needed; 6 = least improvement needed).

1. Introduction . . . . ☐
2. Topic transitions . . . . ☐
3. Headlines . . . . ☐
4. Using silences . . . . ☐
5. Leading into the summary . . . . ☐
6. The summary itself . . . . ☐

CHAPTER 5
Delivery

Effective business briefers communicate clearly, efficiently and informatively. The advice in this chapter will help you do the same.

Brevity, clarity and understandability

If you cannot express yourself simply and succinctly then the people you brief will find it much harder to follow, appreciate and act on what you say. Brevity, clarity and understandability can all be enhanced by:

- delivering each of your points in one or two pithy sentences (without reducing the quality of your points or sounding blunt or terse).
- using short (single breath) sentences without any complicating clauses or digressions.
- making specific, explicit and detailed points to minimize misunderstandings.
- avoiding long words, unnecessary repetition, jargon and any technical terms that may be unfamiliar to your listeners.
- striving at all times to use the most accurate word, not just the first word that comes into your head.
- eliminating all redundant words, unfinished sentences (eg 'I would just..., I would just like to add ...') and lazy speech mannerisms (particularly 'uhms' and 'erms').
- leaving short (ie 3–5 second) pauses after your key points for people to digest what you have said.

It is not unusual to find around 50–75 per cent of what is said by an average business briefer to be non-relevant or even totally unnecessary to the briefing being given. Not only does such verbal inefficiency waste valuable time and energy, it will almost certainly tax the patience of your listeners and could, in turn, seriously compromise their subsequent performance.

Exercise 1: Here is a real-life example of a point that was poorly expressed by a manager briefing his staff in a hi-fi store:

'Erm, just a couple of things: The..., in the book... the book I've got in my hand here... there are..., so that we all know what promotional offers are on the..., erm, our company's produced like a ..., every week, they produce these things... memos... which tell us, whether the promotions on, whether it's finished, that way what the current promotion is so we actually know, like the... the er, the five f... free audio cassette tapes ends, y'know, this weekend and things like that, so that we actually know. So it's in here. So if you're unsure, like, whether the f... the free ABC five cassette pack on selected personal stereos is still on it'll tell you here. Erm, or free carrying cases or whatever. It should tell you all there. So, that's that.' [134 words]

What is this briefer actually trying to say? Rewrite this sequence, using the advice in the bulleted points above, so that both: i) the point this briefer is attempting to make, and ii) the example he provides are expressed more clearly.

Point:_____

_____

_____

_____

Example: _____

_____

_____

_____

How many words have you used? Compare your versions with mine on page 40. Compare your versions with mine on page 40.
    Your briefing should be spoken in a relaxed, friendly and 'conversational' tone of voice. To boost people's interest and understanding, try to deliver your points by modulating your:

- **speed**. Speak slower when you are saying something serious or making a particularly important point; speak faster when you want to display enthusiasm, commitment, urgency and passion.
- **tone**. Alter the character of your voice depending on whether you are being serious, factual, critical, inspirational, friendly, disappointed, etc. Above all, avoid speaking in a flat, dull monotone or through a fixed, inane smile.
- **rhythm**. Deliver your information in noticeably different sized chunks to vary the pace of what you say. Any long sentences should be followed by a short sentence, etc.
- **amplitude**. Use a relatively *louder* voice to stress *all* your *key words* in *each* and *every* sentence you speak. Do not forget that you can also emphasize a point by speaking in a relatively softer voice and by timing special hand gestures and head and upper body movements to coincide with the most important words in your points.

Aim to keep making brief eye contact with everyone present. Look *into* their eyes and not only *at* their faces when you do so. The best places to do this are in the pauses you leave after completing your key points. Aside from helping you to chunk your information into discrete units of talk, these pauses will also provide you with an opportunity to gauge your listeners' reactions to what you have just said. Resist the temptation to rush to glance at your notes (to find your next point) at these junctures and, whenever possible, avoid speaking while looking at your notes.

In terms of your body language you should refrain from doing anything which distracts people away from what you are saying, such as:

- Pacing about like a caged animal.
- Repetitive or overly theatrical gestures.
- Fidgeting with your hands.
- Touching your hair, neck, parts of your face or upper torso (including your tie, collar, cuffs, etc).

Most of these mannerisms are a result of tension or a lack of confidence in what you are saying. Calmness, confidence and credibility are conveyed through a body language characterized by slowness and stillness. (But this does not mean you have to behave like a sloth or stand rigid when delivering your briefing – just stand erect, hold your head high, keep your hands out of your pockets and minimize all unnecessary movement and 'visual loudness'.)

Dealing with problems of inattentiveness

Stifled yawns, glazed expressions and wandering eyes are sure-fire signs that people's attention has begun to wander. Here are three techniques to help you regain and hold people's attention while delivering your briefing:

1. **Unexpected silences**. Stop talking as soon as you realize people's attention is beginning to wander. Be abrupt: Stop mid-sentence (mid–word is even better) – and remain silent until everyone is looking at you. (They will invariably do this out of a curiosity to see what 'problem' has arisen.) Then – and *only* then – continue your briefing, doing so from the beginning of the sentence you had started before you interrupted yourself. You can achieve the same effect by deliberately stuttering.

2. **Random and unpredictable eye contact**. The brief eye contact you periodically establish with each person present should be made in a random way. Do not, for instance, systematically scan your gaze from the person on your extreme left via everyone else until you reach the person on your extreme right. Be unpredictable. The people at your briefing will not then know when they will be next required to meet and 'return' your gaze and, as such, will be more likely continue looking at you and (at least appear to) be attentive for your briefing.

3. **Random and unpredictable questions**. By tagging an unexpected question to the end of a statement you make (eg '. . . right?' '. . . *okay* Mr Bennet?'). Your listeners will not know precisely when or to whom you will spring your next question and will therefore be more likely to remain on the alert throughout your briefing.

The earlier you react to these situations the quicker you will create a climate which shows you expect nothing less than the full, undivided attention of everyone present for your entire briefing.

Providing high quality information and advice

All points, particularly your most important points and those which are likely to be contentious should be fully explained and supported with facts, statistics and examples whenever possible.

One of the best ways of delivering an informative briefing is by increasing the quantity and quality of the advice you provide to assist the people you brief to accomplish their tasks. Unfortunately, because effective practical advice is one of the most difficult types of information to provide it is also the least likely to be given.

The quantity and quality of topics in briefings
The number of topics in a briefing does not always determine the actual duration or the quality of that briefing. In a study of a sample of 20 daily business briefings given by retail store managers to their sales staff, the longest briefing (lasting nearly 10 minutes) contained 8 topics whereas the shortest briefing (lasting under 1 minute) contained 9 topics. What accounted for the different length of these 20 briefings was not the type of topics raised by individual briefers but the level of detail of the information they provided. Indeed, it seemed that quantity was directly related to quality. Those briefers who delivered detailed information and instructions, provided the most explanations and gave the best practical advice tended to hold longer briefings and were rated as the most effective briefers by their staff.

Source: Colin Clark (1997), 'The Communication and Motivation Skills Employed by Retail Store Managers During Morning Briefings'. *Research Report.*

The sentiment of phrases like: 'If you need any help then all you need to do is come and see me and ask for it' is fine, but not when it is a substitute for providing the information and advice people require to accomplish their tasks and targets. Think of some advice you have recently given to the people you brief. Repeat that advice to yourself. Now add one of the following phrases:

- 'To be more specific . . .'
- 'In other words: . . .'
- 'That is to say: . . .'
- 'So, to give an actual example: . . .'
- 'What that means is: . . .'

. . . and complete your own sentence. What you force yourself to say next will invariably expand on and improve the quality, and usefulness, of the advice you provide.

Visual aids, handouts and confirming notes

With the advent of modern presentation software packages it has never been easier to create high quality charts, graphs and tables as illustrations for a speech. Even so, many business briefers would be much more effective if they spent more of their valuable preparation time working on the spoken content and quality of their briefings rather than producing professional looking visual aids. No matter how professional your slides, overhead transparencies, etc. may look they can never compensate for a poorly expressed and amateurish briefing. Moreover, visual aids are always liable to disrupt the flow of your speech and break the vital bond of direct contact between you and your audience. In sum, they must always be used with care.

Using visual aids is a particularly good idea if you have to talk about something that is highly complex or is figuratively detailed (eg a set of accounts, a route map or a table of statistics) and when you need to direct people's attention to specific places on a chart, etc. Before you decide to use these materials, you should be absolutely certain that what you intend to display will significantly clarify, reinforce and enhance people's understanding of the point you are making.

Here are two contrasting – bad and good – examples of the use of visual materials in a speech. Imagine someone is delivering a presentation on how to brief people more effectively. This person begins one point by saying:

In an *ideal* business briefing, people's level of interest and attention is *constantly high* from the beginning to the end of the briefing.

. . . and then shows the following slide:

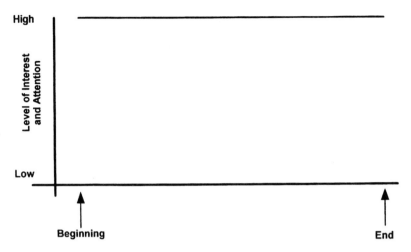

Figure 3 *Level of interest and attention during an ideal business briefing*

... then adds:

> In a *typical* business briefing people's level of interest and attention often *starts high* but then quickly and progressively *declines*.

... and shows the next slide:

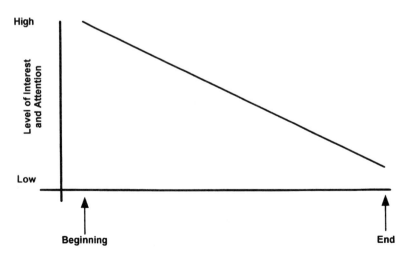

Figure 4 *Level of interest and attention during a typical business briefing*

These slides *do not* significantly add to, clarify or enhance people's understanding of the point being made. They simply repeat it, albeit in a visually simple way. This point could have been more effectively made by the briefer using simple hand gestures to visually 'paint' the two graph lines in the air. (It also would also have saved that person approximately 40 minutes in slide preparation time.) Here is a better example. The same speaker begins another point in the same presentation by saying:

> *Don't* bury your most important point (represented by the letter 'P' in the following slide) in the body of your briefing.

. . . and then shows the following slide:

```
DODODODODODODODOD
ODODODODODODODODO
DODODODODODODODOD
ODODODODODODODODO
DODODODODODODODOD
ODODODODODODODODO
DODODODODODOPODOD
ODODODODODODODODO
DODODODODODODODOD
ODODODODODODODODO
```

. . . then says:

> . . . It will be *easily missed* and *difficult to remember*. Make it the VERY FIRST thing you mention.

. . . and shows the next slide:

```
PODODODODODODODOD
DODODODODODODODOD
ODODODODODODODODO
DODODODODODODODOD
ODODODODODODODODO
DODODODODODODODOD
ODODODODODODODODO
DODODODODODODODOD
ODODODODODODODODO
DODODODODODODODOD
```

. . . then adds:

> . . . and EMPHASIZE it to make it hard to forget and impossible to ignore.

. . . and shows the final slide:

These slides *do* significantly add to, clarify and enhance people's understanding of the point being made. Indeed, they literally provide a graphic and convincing illustration of that point. The letter 'P' is very difficult for people to *visually* distinguish in the first slide; it becomes much easier to distinguish when it is placed in the 'first point' position, and even easier when it is emphasized – exactly like a main point should be when delivered *verbally*.

When preparing and using visual aids:

- Never show a chart, etc and then simply repeat what is on that chart.
- Make your illustrations simple and unambiguous. Graphics need to be graphic, vivid, bold and striking.
- Keep the number of typefaces, fonts and colours you use to a minimum.
- Restrict the amount of visual material you use. Use illustrations only for your most important, key points.
- If you intend to use a flip-chart or whiteboard, write down what is going to be on it *before* your briefing.
- Do not turn away from your audience when you are using a visual aid.

Any visually displayed material that takes people longer than about ten seconds to digest is probably better given as a handout. Distribute your handouts only when they are needed – you need everyone's full attention throughout your briefing and such material can be distracting. Handouts have a habit of encouraging people to read what you have written rather than to listen to what you are saying. Similarly, do not continue delivering your briefing whilst your handouts are being distributed.

If the subject matter of your briefing is especially complex or you need to mention many facts and figures, then consider providing everyone present with a set of notes confirming what you have said. These notes will also be useful for anyone who was unable to attend your briefing. Be aware, though, that if you regularly distribute elaborate confirming notes they may be treated by those you brief as a substitute for listening to or attending your briefing.

Answers to Exercise 1 page 32
The point:
'If you're unsure about the start and finish dates of any of our special offers or promotions or what our current promotion is, this book tells you.' [27 words]

The example:
'For instance, it states that the free ABC 5 pack audio-cassette offer on selected personal stereos ends this weekend.' [20 words]

. . . and you would have cut out nearly two thirds of the words used by this briefer.

CHAPTER 6
Impact

> If you drew a line on a graph showing people's level of interest over the length of a brilliant briefing, it would be horizontal and at the highest possible point, from beginning to end. In an exceptional or even useful briefing it would still be horizontal, but obviously not as high. In the boring briefings we've received recently that line would begin on a low point and then plummet as soon as the site manager opened his mouth.
>
> **Civil engineer**

Although you may have a captive audience for your business briefing this does not mean that people will always be captivated by what you say. Indeed, even when you deliver an understandable and highly informative briefing you still cannot guarantee that what you say will be remembered or even listened to. You never can. However, what you *can* attempt to do – particularly for the most important parts of your briefing – is to use the special techniques contained in this chapter to boost their impact and memorability.

You can add impact to your briefings by *reinforcing* and/or *repackaging* what you say.

Reinforcing what you say

Here you add impact by adding particular types of words or phrases to what you were already going to say.

Repetition

Repeating key words and phrases is one of the easiest ways to reinforce a point:

- . . . it must, must, *must* be finished by the end of the evening.
- It's *everybody's* responsibility, not just one or two of you, *everybody's* responsibility.
- We've got to do *something* and we've got to do something *quick*.

Whenever you make an especially important point do not forget to emphasize just how important it is. Many effective briefers repeat their main point *three times* – immediately after they first mention their main point and also as their first and final point in their end of briefing summary.

Alliteration and poetics

You can inject life into the most mundane of information by employing words that share the same first letter or similar vowel sounds within a single sentence. Sentences that have a rhyming quality sound particularly melodic and easy on the ear:

Ordinary	Impact Enhanced
We had an excellent Sunday yesterday.	We had a *'Simply Superb Sunday'* yesterday.
We're here to help our customers.	We're here to help not to harangue or harass our customers.
It's got to be finished quickly.	It's got to be finished swiftly and surely and certainly.

Superlatives

Most briefers strengthen key words by prefacing them with strengthening adjectives such as 'very', 'really' 'quite', etc (eg 'good' becomes *'very* good'). You can boost the power and persuasiveness of a point by using words that express your point in the strongest possible way.

Ordinary	Impact Enhanced
We are at the bottom of our sales league this week.	This week we are *well and truly* at the *very rock bottom* of our sales league. We are *absolutely nowhere*.
I've never seen that before.	I've *never ever* seen that before in my *entire* life.
That strategy works best.	That strategy works better than any other possible or conceivable alternative.

Repackaging what you say

Here you reorganize what you would ordinarily say and deliver it in an almost totally different way.

Lists of three items

Points that are delivered in lists of three items have an almost mystical aura of power and persuasiveness about them. They sound complete, comprehensive and, above all, convincing – as if the three items you selected for your list could be the only possible items in that list:

Ordinary	Impact Enhanced
Let's have a fantastic day.	Let's have a [1] *bubbling*, [2] *sizzling*, [3] *fantastic* day.
We need to be doing more business.	We need to be [1] *pulling the deals out of the hat*, [2] *sticking them in the till*, and [3] *doing more business*.
Yes, I know we've got problems with our performance targets, but ...	Yes, [1] I *know* our performance target's *unrealistic*, [2] yeah, we keep saying it's being *looked at*, [3] yeah we keep saying it's *changing*, but. . .

On this basis, lists containing *more* than three items are an excellent way to hammer home a point by overstating that point.

Ordinary	Impact Enhanced
In terms of our general performance, we are bottom of our district.	We're [1] *bottom* on call-out, [2] *bottom* on sales, [3] *bottom* against target, [4] *bottom* against customer contacts, [5] *bottom against everything.*
I don't want to see any dust anywhere.	Every single [1] *nook,* [2] *cranny,* [3] *product,* [4] *wire,* [5] *ticket,* [6] *the whole lot,* it all has to be *spotlessly clean.*

Contrasts

Contrasts are 'loaded' comparisons. They are created by juxtaposing two related items of information in explicit opposition and contradiction to one another. They are one of the most efficient and effective ways of accentuating a difference and adding drama to a point.

Ordinary	Impact Enhanced
We missed 38 sales opportunities yesterday.	We had [1] 43 sales opportunities yesterday and [2] only 5 were taken up.
Those plants in the small nursery only cost £1.99 now.	Those plants were [1] £5 each last week, weren't they? They're [2] only £1.99 now.
We're not taking as much money as we took last week.	. . . we only took [1] *five* thousand on Sunday and *five* thousand on Monday. This time *last week* we did [2] *thirteen* thousand on a Monday *alone.*

Contrasts are synergistic. Each element or 'side' of the contrast, when combined and opposed generates an effect that is stronger and more persuasive than each element could generate on its own. When you use contrasts you need to ensure that your listeners can easily appreciate the comparison you are making. The impact of a contrast between two different prices, for instance, will be much reduced if one of those prices is given in a different and unfamiliar currency. A short silence between each element of the contrast will also heighten impact.

With these basic rhetorical building bricks it is possible to build a great deal of high impact points. The following sequence contains examples of almost all the techniques mentioned above:

What about lost sales? It can happen in a *busy* showroom, it can happen in a *slow* showroom, it can happen *absolutely anytime*. But, *but*, if we keep approaching *each* and *every* customer at *each* and *every* possible opportunity it'll *never ever* have to happen again.

Exercise 2: How many examples of the techniques mentioned in this chapter so far can you find in the sequence above? (Clue: There are over 30.) Check your findings with the answers on page 48.

Visual words
You can breathe life and energy into the blandest of points by employing vivid action words and descriptions to plant hard to forget pictures of your points in the minds of the people you brief.

Ordinary	Impact Enhanced
We're expecting 20,000 people to attend Saturday's demonstration.	. . . that's the equivalent of over 300 double-decker buses full of protesters.
It's a really hot day today.	Glorious sunshine's beating down outside there.
John and Jane tried their very best to solve that problem.	John and Jane fought like devils possessed to solve that problem.

The key here is to use words or examples that dramatically illustrate and animate your point. Appeal to people's senses.

Exercise 3: Can you guess how the following three points were animated by their respective briefers?

'I don't want to lose any more customers in our shop.' Store Manager

'The measures I suggest we take will help safeguard food hygiene at every stage, from the farmer to the consumer.' Food Hygienist

'Senior managers should be blamed more for the poor performances of their staff.' Personnel Officer

See page 49 for the answers.

Clichés

Tired speech creates tired listeners. Banish all vague, over-used and empty expressions such as:

- let's go for it;
- we need to be more competitive;
- we're heading in the right direction;

... from your briefings. Clichés like these are a very poor substitute for accurate and enlightening information and are one of the most successful antidotes to memorability and effectiveness. If you must use clichés then do so only when you deliberately want to sound tired and over-familiar (eg when people have ignored or have failed to act on something you have previously said) because that's inevitably how what you say will sound.

Humour

Humour, and even the occasional joke, can supercharge the impact of an otherwise mundane topic or point and increase the memorability of what you say. It is an excellent way to relax everyone at the beginning of a briefing and for building a rapport during your briefing. But humour can also be used to manage other important and often problematic tasks such as:

Saying difficult things in a tactful and non-threatening way:
In one retail company, store managers were told to discourage their sales teams from spending their free time talking at the cash desks as it seemed to be discouraging some shoppers from buying. One store manager tried to gain the compliance of his staff by threatening them:

> Except for the two cashiers that are meant to be on there, *keep off the cash desk*. Anybody who doesn't will *definitely* get reported to X [the regional manager].

Another store manager used humour:

Briefer: 'Unless you're a cashier or you're serving a customer, *keep away from the cash desk*. If you *can't*, I'll get a barbed wire fence put round it and plug it into the electricity socket. *That'll keep you all off it!*'
Staff: [Laughter]
Briefer: '*Okay?*'
Staff: Yeah.

. . . and obtained exactly the same level of co-operation but without resorting to heavy-handed tactics or alienating her staff.

Defusing tension before or after raising a controversial topic or issue
Briefer: 'Our performance has been so wretched recently I spent all weekend thinking of an urgent solution. Here it is: [Pause] we all need to eat more 'Weetabix' for our breakfasts!'
Staff: [Laughter]
Briefer: 'Of course, as well as doing that we need to . . .'[makes serious point]

Highlighting or adding strength to a point

I'm *very very* impressed with all the extra effort you've been making over the last two weeks. Our bread sales have risen so quickly we'll all be suffering from high altitude nosebleeds very soon.

Here is one way you can create your own humour:

● Think of the (serious) point you are intending to make (eg, 'The main task today is cleaning our wine cellar. It's filthy.')
● . . . then give an over-exaggerated example which vividly illustrates your point or a positive or negative consequence of it: (eg 'I'm breathing in so much dust down there I'll have developed lung cancer by next week.')

. . . add them together, put a short pause between them and you have your humorous point. The more vivid and absurd the over-exaggeration the better the reaction you are likely to obtain. The beauty of this technique is that you don't have to be 'naturally funny' to be able to make people laugh; only creative. (You may also have noticed that all three of the previous examples could have been created using exactly the same technique.)
To make the most of humour you should use it:

● only when it will add power to the point you are making. Your humorous material should never swamp a serious message;
● in addition to the point you are making, rather than a complete substitute for it;
● sparingly and appropriately. The line between being funny and sounding flippant and unconcerned can be a very narrow one.

Be particularly careful if you attempt to poke fun at the people you brief. Even when they laugh along with you they may not always appreciate a joke made at their expense. Finally, only start your next point when everyone has finished laughing and has settled down. If you take care to do this you will find that the information you deliver next is also likely to be listened to with a greater degree of attentiveness than is usual.

Warning: All of the techniques mentioned in this chapter must never be overused. (The simplest of these techniques to master – eg repetition – are also the easiest to overuse.) A briefing should *never* be a triumph of style over substance. Impact and effectiveness are not always one and the same thing. Aim for added impact only when you feel certain that your points i) would not be compromised; and/or ii) would otherwise not be fully appreciated, understood, remembered or acted on.

Answers to Exercise 2 page 45
I found 36.

Emphasis: *'busy'*, *'slow'*, *'absolutely anytime'*, *'each'* (×2), *'every'* (×2) and *'never ever'*.

Alliteration:
'slow showroom'
'absolutely anytime'
'each and every' (×2)
'have to happen'

Repetition:
'it can happen' (×3)
'but' (×2)
'showroom' (×2)
'each and every' (×2)

Poetics:
'slow showroom'
'never ever'
'have to happen'

Strengtheners/Maximizers:
'absolutely anytime'
'each and every' (×2)
'every *possible* opportunity'
'never'
'ever'

Contrasts:
Busy/slow showroom.
Losing/not losing sales.

3-part lists, etc:
i) 'busy showroom...'
ii) 'slow showroom'
iii) 'anytime.'
iv) The series of three phrases in the final sentence.

Scoring:

30 plus	*Excellent*. Now all you have to do is put these techniques into practice.
20–30	*Good*. You need to improve your ability to recognise these skills before you can use them to their best effect.
Under 20	*Poor*. You may benefit from reading the first part of this chapter again.

Answers to Exercise 3 page 45

i) I don't want to **watch any deals walking out the door**.

ii) It will help safeguard food hygiene standards at every stage, **from the plough to the plate**.

iii) **A fish rots from its head**; so, too, does a typical company.

CHAPTER 7
Motivation

Whenever you feel you need to encourage, urge, cajole or otherwise motivate the people you brief to accomplish their tasks or targets the first question you should ask yourself is not 'How?' but 'Why?' Your answer will almost always point to one of the following problems.

- A fundamental problem within your organization – poor wages or working conditions, understaffing, overworking, ever increasing performance targets, etc. (As this type of problem will often be outside your control it is not addressed in this book).
- A problem with the amount or the quality of information, resources, and support you provide the people you brief to help them accomplish their tasks and targets. (This type of problem is dealt with in the other chapters of this book).
- A problem with the people you brief having negative attitudes or low expectations about being able to accomplish what, objectively, are reasonable and achievable tasks and targets.

This chapter provides advice on how you can deal with the last of these problems and inspire the people you brief to maintain or improve their level of performance.

Negative attitudes and expectations

These can strongly influence people's level of motivation, particularly when people have low levels of confidence in their ability or high expectations of failure with regard to the tasks or targets you have set. The following exercise provides a vivid, if unusual, illustration of this idea:

Exercise 4: Is it possible to cover all nine dots in Figure 5 below by using only four straight lines?

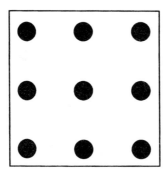

Figure 5

See page 56 for the answer.

This exercise illustrates how people often create non-existent barriers which limits their thinking and compromises their ability to accomplish achievable things. In this exercise there was no rule specifying how long each of the four lines should be. However, because many people mentally limit the length of these lines to being no more than three dots long they are thereby unable to solve the puzzle. The square border surrounding the nine dots also encourages (but does not constrain) a limit on the length of lines used. Use this exercise on the people you brief as a first step to convincing them of the power of negative attitudes and low self-expectations on their performance.

The most common way business briefers attempt to inspire the people they brief and, more specifically, to deal with negative attitudes and low expectations is with short and simple 'rah-rah' phrases, such as:

- Come on guys and girls! I *know* you can do it.
- You *can* achieve it, *if* you believe in yourself and *if* you put your minds to it.
- Let's get out there and behave like *winners*.

Clichés like these, especially when they are used on their own, are actually one of the least effective ways to motivate people. The fact that they are often delivered at the very end of a business briefing only reaffirms why they are invariably treated by the people who have to hear them as an uninspiring afterthought, which they usually are. By far the best way to verbally motivate the people you brief is by providing everyone with all the information and advice they require to accomplish the objectives you set.

But sometimes even this is not enough. For example, many recipients of business briefings have difficulty in accepting objectives that entail changing established patterns of behaviour or appear to be particularly difficult to achieve. Generally this is because of the increased feelings of uncertainty such objectives bring with them. Two of the best ways to reduce this uncertainty and to motivate people to accept such challenges with enthusiasm are: first by drawing a parallel between your new objective and some current behaviour or attitude that the people you brief already find acceptable:

> We've just had another of our drivers prosecuted for not wearing a seat-belt and I want him to be the last. I know it's inconvenient when you have to keep getting in and out of your car. But, if nothing else, think about your own safety. You don't fail to wear a seat-belt in a plane, do you? Then why avoid wearing one when you're driving? Statistically you're far more likely to be injured or killed in a car than in a plane.

Second, by pointing out a previous occasion where the same type of challenge has already been faced and overcome by the people you are briefing:

> Anna, up to three weeks ago you were actually hitting 73 per cent or more of your target *all the time*. Nothing's changed, has it? If you did it then you can also do it now, okay?

> Jane, I want to see you coming out of the lingerie area of the store more often, to help out in women's clothing and children's footwear. You can't guarantee that you're always going to get lots of big sales in your own section. Now I know you, you *can* sell footwear, you *can* sell women's clothing, you've *already* sold *plenty* of those linen dresses we got in recently. *I* know and *you* know you've got the time and the talent to do it.

The way you package your information can also enhance peoples' level of motivation. Chapter 6, on 'Impact', will be of help to you in this respect. The following example shows one of the most common ways business briefers package their information in a demotivating way. A positive point (A) is followed by the main, and often demotivating, point (B):

(A)We actually managed to increase our plant production rate by four per cent over the last quarter so thank you all for that. (B) But now we need to now to double that figure from four per cent to eight per cent.

This combination of 'good news – bad news' is regularly cited by recipients of briefings as being demoralizing. A far better way to package information like this is to reverse the order of the sentences and deliver your positive point second:

(B) We need to increase our plant production rate by four per cent in the next quarter. (A) We've done it before – in the last quarter – surely we can build on that success and do it again?

Tone as a motivator

If you do not look or sound confident that the people you brief will achieve their objectives they are hardly likely to feel confident themselves. So, whenever possible, be positive and upbeat. Set the tone of your briefing immediately, by making your introduction or your first topic a positive one:

Good afternoon everybody. I've got *fantastic* news about our sales. There's *glorious* sunshine outside and we're having a *brilliant* week so far. We're 29.8 per cent above our target, which is £31,502. *Right?* Which means we're £1432 *up* on last week, and we're on for a *fever pitched fortnight, right*, to end the week off with a *fantastic finish*.

When people attempt to motivate others they almost always make some form of positive or negative appeal to strengthen their motivation attempt.

Positive appeals highlight the advantages of doing something. These appeals use rewards and incentives and invoke things like personal pride and self-respect and security to motivate:

From today you'll receive a bonus payment on any XYZ unit you sell. So, if you are one of the lucky people to sell them, you will get twenty pounds extra in your wage packets for that. And that's *official*. And you can take that straight home and put it in the bank, *all right?*

Negative appeals highlight the negative consequences of failing to do something. These appeals use threats and sanctions and invoke things like fear and tension to motivate:

> Those people who don't make their target figure this month *will* be reported to the area manager, and you know what that means, don't you? *Everybody's* job is on the line!

In the vast majority of business briefing situations positive appeals will be the most successful motivators. Negative appeals should only be employed in crisis situations; if even then. Negative appeals are more effective when only a moderate amount of fear or tension is induced. Increased levels of fear rarely result in increased levels of either motivation or performance. The power of a positive appeal can be enhanced by getting people to visualize their success and by detailing any benefits that will come to them if they succeed:

> There is *absolutely nothing* to worry about. You can be sure, as *I* am sure, that if you do your job half as well as you did it on last week's training exercise that, by Friday evening, we'll all be sitting in the pub sipping a shandy and smiling proudly at your deserved success. Just put your training into action, nothing more, nothing less, and by next Monday I *personally* guarantee you'll all be taken on as full-time staff.

Praising and criticizing as a motivator

It is easy to underrate the power of praise and even criticism as a motivator. If people have performed well then do not forget to give recognition where it is due for that performance. It is worth being appreciative of effort, even when it is was misdirected or unproductive. But do not indulge in empty praise. It is quite obvious that if you repeatedly use negative terms such as 'poor', 'appalling', 'terrible', 'rubbish' when assessing things like the performance of the people you brief that, eventually, this will have a counterproductive effect on their morale and performance. What is not so obvious is that the same negative effect can result from overusing highly positive terms such as 'brilliant', 'fantastic', 'exceptional', etc – especially when they are not justified. Also, by overusing terms like these, you will only incite people to think that the other things you say may be equally hollow and insincere.

Criticism, when warranted, can be a highly effective motivator but it must be used with tact and sensitivity. This is when an understanding of the individual personalities of the people you brief would be very helpful. Some individuals are easily deflated by the mildest of criticism whilst others will be spurred to greater heights by nothing but the strongest. There is one rule that you should almost always adhere to: praise people in public but punish individuals in private.

The following exercise tests your knowledge of which type of criticism will usually motivate groups of people the most when admonishing them for, say, their poor performance.

Exercise 5: Rate the following criticisms in terms of their relative ability to motivate the people being criticized. (1 = most effective motivator; 5 = least effective motivator.)

1. *'We* let *ourselves* down yesterday.' .... ☐

2. 'You let [name of *organization*] down yesterday.' ..... ☐

3. 'You let *me* down yesterday.' .... ☐

4. 'You let *your colleagues* down yesterday.' .... ☐

5. 'You let *yourselves* down yesterday.' .... ☐

See page 57 for the answers.

Typically, people who work in groups are most likely to be motivated to avoid letting down their colleagues and other people with whom they have a close, personal and direct working relationship. Any motivational appeals you make, criticisms included, should try to take account of these factors. Conversely, motivational strategies which appeal to distant and impersonal things such as loyalty to an organization are often far less successful.

Whenever you praise or criticize individuals in front of their colleagues the other people present will, of course, be listening to what you are saying. Use this opportunity therefore to provide useful information for the benefit of everyone present about the way in which either the praised behaviour was achieved:

Junior, you made £1725 worth of sales yesterday. £899 of that was for a single sale. *Fantastic!* Look everybody, one major sale and, *bang!* you hit your bonus target for this week. Tell us all how you did it Junior.

. . . or the way in which the criticized behaviour can be avoided:

We are simply not contacting enough shoppers in our store. On seven occasions yesterday I noticed salespeople walking right past shoppers who were giving off all the classic signs of wanting to be served. For the guilty people among you here is a short refresher on the type of shopper body language of which you need to be aware...

Anything which makes people's tasks and targets easier to achieve is likely to motivate. If you must criticize individuals in front of their colleagues try to focus on the problem itself in an indirect and impersonal way rather than on the personal failings of the individual being criticized.

The level of motivation of the people you brief can be the decisive factor between the success and failure of your objectives. When you deliver your business briefings remember that it is far easier to demotivate people than it is to motivate them; and it is far harder to repair the damage created by a demotivating briefing than it is to deliver an effective and inspirational one.

Exercise 4 page 51
Yes!

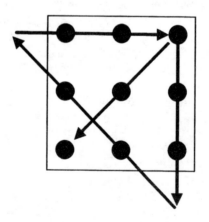

Exercise 5 page 55

CRITICISM	MOTIVATIONAL RATING
1	3
2	5
3	4
4	1
5	2

CHAPTER 8
Informal Feedback

Not all feedback takes the form of information you explicitly ask for or receive from the people you brief. A large amount of highly significant information can be obtained informally by discreetly monitoring people while you are briefing them. This chapter describes two of the most important types of informal feedback you are likely to receive and how to interpret it when you receive it.

Silent feedback

The body language of the people you brief is one of the most important sources of informal feedback. It can provide vital clues about what they think about you and your briefing as well as what they think about each other. But real-life body language is far more difficult to interpret accurately than many business briefers imagine. A person whose eyes are closed may be asleep, bored or concentrating very hard; someone who is nodding when you are talking may be signalling their continued agreement or revealing that their attention has wandered; someone who is scratching their nose may be showing signs of tension or merely relieving an itch.

However, this does not mean that it is impossible to accurately interpret non-verbal behaviour. Each particular kind of gesture, body position or look has its own ideal type. Knowing these ideal types will help you recognize when people are responding positively and appreciatively; they will also help you detect any behaviour that deviates from these ideals and is likely, therefore, to signify something negative and potentially problematic. The table below outlines a range of ideal and negative forms of body language commonly displayed by recipients of business briefings:

BODY LANGUAGE	IDEAL	NEGATIVE
Body Position		
Alignment	Head, body and legs facing directly towards you.	Head or body or legs not facing towards you; head and body facing in markedly different directions to each other.
Proximity	Standing or sitting close to you but not uncomfortably so. Any significant movement towards you.	Distant from you. Any significant movement away from you.
Posture	Open	Closed
General	Relaxed but alert.	Slouched and unresponsive; restless and fidgeting.
Arms	Uncrossed and akimbo.	Crossed over the chest; held behind the back or on top of head; hands in pockets.
Legs	Relatively stationary and together; open, but not wide apart.	Crossed and tense; continually shifting position; tapping of feet.
Hands	Relatively stationary on desk or (if standing up) hanging by the side of body outside pockets.	Persistent drumming of fingers; fiddling or wringing of hands; 'auto-involvement's' (ie self-touching of the ears, temples, chin, inside of a collar, shirt cuffs, etc).

BODY LANGUAGE	IDEAL	NEGATIVE
Face		
Gaze and eye contact	Readiness to return and (briefly) hold eye contact.	Persistently averted eyes; markedly short and irregular periods of eye contact; easily distracted; prolonged, intimidating eye-contact.
Facial expressions	Receptive and animated.	Blank and unresponsive; any form of staring.
Head.	Facing towards you. Frequent head nods at appropriate points of another person's speech.	Facing away from you; shakes of the head; slow and minimal head nods; no head nods; nodding at inappropriate points.

Likewise, monitoring how, where and with whom the people you brief sit (or stand) can also provide you with many important clues, particularly about the existence of any interpersonal conflicts or cliques that may exist. Figures 6, 7 and 8 show plan views of the ideal seating or standing arrangements in the three most common environments where briefings are conducted: around a table; in a lecture room; and in an open space where everyone is standing. You can notice in each case that the people being briefed are evenly spaced from each other and their heads and bodies are aligned towards the briefer (ie 'B'):

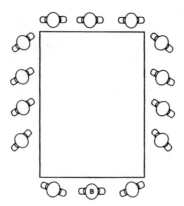

Figure 6 *Ideal seating arrangement around a table*

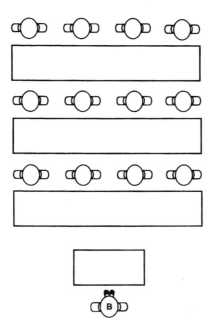

Figure 7 *Ideal seating arrangement in a lecture room*

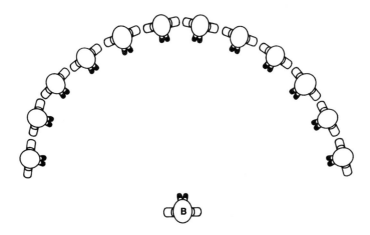

Figure 8 *Ideal standing arrangement in an open space*

As before, these ideal types are positive signals. What you should continuously be looking for are any potentially problematic deviations from these ideals, such as the following:

- Anyone who avoids standing or sitting near to you or directly in front of you, where their behaviour can more easily be scrutinized and anyone who may be hiding behind someone else.
- Anyone who is not fully facing you. This often indicates low interest and involvement.
- People who congregate together in small self-contained and distant groups. This may be a sign of a clique.
- People who regularly sit or stand just a little too close to you for comfort. Even if they are not sycophants they may be perceived as such by others present.
- Anyone who is sitting or standing on their own. These people may be finding it difficult to fit into your staff team.

Exercise 6: Figures 9, 10 and 11 show examples of deviations from the ideal seating or standing arrangements shown in Figures 6, 7 and 8:

Figure 9 *Deviation from ideal seating arrangement around a table*

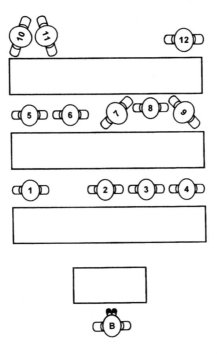

Figure 10 *Deviation from ideal seating arrangement in a lecture room*

Figure 11 *Deviation from an ideal standing arrangement in an open space*

- Which individuals, if any, *may* be a) too close to you and b) the least involved or interested in what you are saying or paying the least attention?
- Which individuals, standing or sitting on their own (but not close to you), *may* not be full members of your team?
- Which groups are *possible* cliques?

See page 66 for the answers.

Informal verbal feedback – interjections

While you are speaking you will often receive short interjections from the people you are briefing (eg 'Mmm', 'Uh huh', 'Okay', 'Right', 'Great', 'Absolutely fantastic', etc). These interjections form a useful barometer of how people feel about what you are saying. Typically, the more frequent and positive and substantive the interjections you receive the better. The following types of interjections are *highly positive*:

Briefer: 'We had a massive delivery of stock yesterday. The shoppers will be fighting each other to buy the gear that's out there now.'
Staff: [Laughter]
Staff no 1: 'We've finally got those brilliant new denims in.'
Briefer: 'Look at those dresses we've received too! And the T-shirts that everybody's been asking about.'
Staff no 2: 'They're *marvellous*!'
Staff no 3: 'Right. *Blimey*!'

The following types of interjections are *positive*:

Briefer: 'We could have a good day today, a bad day tomorrow but a great day the day after that. In our restaurant *it's totally unpredictable*.'
Staff no 1: 'Yeah.'
Staff no 2: 'Exactly.'
Briefer: 'We *know* there's never any pattern to it; we *know* we can't control how many people come in and how much they eat and drink.'
Staff no 3: 'True.'
Briefer: 'But I think, if you put your minds to it, we *can* make *some* things happen. We made it happen yesterday.'
Staff no 3: 'Right.'

Staff no 2: 'We did.'
Briefer: 'So, well done everyone!'

The following types of interjections are usually *negative*:

Briefer: 'We had a much better week last week. *That's* good to say, isn't it?'
Staff no 1: 'Mm.'
Briefer: 'I'll read the results out. We took £22,261.'
Staff no 2: 'Oh.'
Briefer: 'Which is 34.6 per cent more than what we took for the same week last year.'
Staff no 3: 'Uh huh.'
Briefer: 'Well *I* thought it was another great week, *why didn't you?* '

To interpret informal feedback accurately you also need to be sensitive to the context within which it occurs:

- Get into the habit of recognizing any before and after changes in a person's body language or any upgrading or downgrading of the relative strength of interjections that are used. One of the best ways of doing this is to think in terms of whether the informal feedback you are receiving changes from positive to negative or vice versa.
- Monitor people's body language and interjections in relation to what is currently being said, particularly after any contentious points are made.

The silent and the small things that often go unnoticed during business briefings are rarely trivial or insignificant. Most briefers have two eyes and two ears and one mouth. It is good advice to accordingly put twice as much effort into watching and listening to and learning from the people you brief rather than talking at them. But remember that informal feedback comprises only *clues* (albeit often very obvious and important clues) to the *possible* thoughts and feelings of the people you brief. When any of these clues indicate possible problems these problems can be dealt with either by discreetly changing what you subsequently say in your briefing or with the more formal means of obtaining feedback that we examine in the next chapter.

Exercise 6 page 64
In Figure 10:
Question 1a: (S1).
Question 1b: (S's 3, 5, 6–9 and 11&12).
Question 2: (S's 3, 4, and 5 particularly S3).
Question 3: (S's 6–9).

In Figure 11:
Question 1a: (other than the people in the first row, none).
Question 1b: (S's 7–9, 10&11; 12).
Question 2: (S12).
Question 3: (S's 7–9).

In Figure 12:
Question 1a: (S1)
Question 1b: (S's 2–5; S8&9; S11&12)
Question 2: (S's 6–10).
Question 3: (S's 2–5).

CHAPTER 9

Formal Feedback

This is the information you obtain as a result of asking for or receiving feedback from the people you brief. Formal feedback usually takes the form of people:

- asking you questions;
- expressing their opinions about and reactions to things you have said during your briefing;
- commenting on their experiences whilst conducting their work tasks or acting on your previous instructions;
- raising problems.

It goes without saying that effective business briefings and success in achieving the objectives set within them are both premised on you receiving and acting on high-quality feedback.

It is worth announcing at the beginning of your briefing when you would prefer to receive any formal feedback. You have three options:

1. Immediately after individual topics or points.
2. If and when any feedback arises.
3. At the end of your briefing.

The first and second options will provide you with feedback when it is most relevant, but feedback at these points can disrupt the flow of your briefing and create time constraints. The main advantage of the third option is that the interruption occurs only at one point, making it far more manageable. However, by the end of your briefing, people may have lost interest in talking about something they would rather have said earlier; or they may have become reluctant to prolong the briefing at this point by making any extensive contributions. If you do decide to use the third option, as most briefers do, then ask for feedback *before* you start your summary. Whatever option you choose you need to allow sufficient time for the feedback you require or expect.

> I've lost count of how many times I've heard my managers end a briefing with the immortal phrase: Any questions? in a tone of voice suggesting they only want to hear one thing from their staff – the word no. It's as if they're living in fear of the type of questions they might be asked to answer.
>
> **Sales Director**

Exercise 7: The following sequence is from the end of a real-life business briefing between a restaurant manager and his kitchen and table staff. In what ways is this manager discouraging his staff from providing any feedback?

Briefer: 'Right, I've run over time. Are those our first diners at the door?'
Staff: 'Mm hmm.'
Briefer: 'Well, let's open up then. Anything else? No? Right. Good. Okay, let's have a great evening.'
[End of briefing]

Check your answers on page 76.

Initiating feedback

The best way to initiate feedback is by asking questions (and lots of them). Start with open-ended questions which encourage people to talk at length and in general terms. Then follow up with more specific questions to clarify and add flesh to the information you received. Follow-up questions should specify what particular detail you require and whether you expect opinions, facts, descriptions, etc. Your questioning should never sound as if you are conducting an interrogation.

Listening to feedback

Active listening involves more than showing you are paying full attention by nodding your head and verbally acknowledging what someone is saying at the appropriate points of their talk. If you are going to make immediate off the cuff decisions based on what you hear you will need to listen properly and have all the relevant facts at hand. To listen actively:

- Give people time and plenty of encouragement to work out precisely what they want to say.
- Adopt positive body language and provide plenty of positive interjections (see Chapter 8).
- Encourage longer, more detailed contributions by nodding your head just before the person speaking is likely to finish their turn. Then you should remain silent. Be careful, however, that you do not force long answers. When people start repeating themselves it often indicates they are struggling to continue speaking.
- Wait until the person speaking has obviously finished before starting to speak yourself. Do not start speaking the moment you think you have the gist of what the other person is saying.
- You should always look at the person who is speaking. While you are doing this you should also try to discreetly monitor the reactions of the others present. This is an excellent way to discover who agrees or disagrees with the person speaking and who does and does not appear to understand what is being said.

Active Listening – A Technique
If you interrupt someone by mistake then immediately stop talking and allow that person to continue. This will leave the unfinished part of your own speech hanging in the air ('I was just ...'; 'Yes, I know what you ...,' etc.). You will probably only have to wait one or two sentences before you get the opportunity to speak again. Never highlight that the other speaker's contribution was a waste of time (even if it was) by restarting with something like: 'As I was saying ...'; 'Anyway, where were we?', etc.

Responding to feedback

Any issues arising from the feedback you receive are best dealt with during your briefing or as soon as possible afterwards. Briefers who have established a history of responding to feedback promptly and positively have a much higher chance of receiving high quality feedback and achieving their objectives. More generally:

- be appreciative of every constructive contribution you receive, even if you disagree with it;
- encourage people to express ideas, opinions and solutions to problems that are different to your own. After all, because they are likely to have different experiences to you they *should* see things differently;
- create precedents that show you don't take personal criticism personally;
- do not reinforce cliques by only asking particular people to speak or by the way you respond to the feedback you receive from them. Treat each and every contribution on its own merits;
- if you do not know an answer to a question or do not know how to deal with an issue someone has raised then say so. You do not need to pretend you know everything;
- encourage the people you brief to listen to and learn from each other.

A feedback action template

Some of the feedback you receive will be on issues you cannot immediately respond to or make a decision upon. In these circumstances far too many briefers say things like: 'Let me look into it' or 'I'll have to get back to you later on that point' and then they forget to do so or they fail to report back about what action they have taken. You can reduce this sort of problem by writing down all the feedback issues that cannot be dealt with immediately on a template similar to that in Figure 12.

Write each issue down as soon as it has been raised (and make sure people see you doing it). Place a copy of what you wrote on a notice-board so that everyone can track what, if anything, is being done. Many briefers automatically incorporate a short action report in their next briefing that deals with the progress of any issues which were raised but not resolved in their previous briefing.

FEEDBACK ACTION PLAN	
Briefer: _____	Date of Briefing: _____
Issues Raised	**Action Taken**

Figure 12 *Feedback action plan template*

A feedback charter for business briefings

Another way to improve the amount and quality of feedback you receive is to compile a list of ground rules about the type of feedback you expect and what the people you brief will receive from you in return. Your charter would probably contain the following recommendations:

The people being briefed will endeavour at all times to:

- attempt to contribute to every briefing;
- provide feedback of the highest possible quality by being candid, accurate, and constructive and avoiding exaggeration;
- present facts and examples to support all major points and arguments;
- listen to contributions made by their colleagues and evaluate those contributions on their own merits, rather than on the basis of who makes them;
- be solution rather than problem orientated;
- state when they do not understand or agree with something that has been said.

71

In return, you will always endeavour to:

- set aside enough time during your briefing for people to ask questions, raise problems and provide feedback;
- judge all contributions on their merits;
- not take any personal criticism personally;
- aim to take feedback related decisions as quickly as possible and by consensus whenever possible;
- provide reasons whenever you disagree with a point raised;
- relay feedback higher up the management chain whenever appropriate.

Print out copies of your charter and have everyone sign it (including yourself). Have private words with anyone whose behaviour transgresses the charter. Make it plain that you expect public criticism from the people you brief whenever you have breached the charter.

Recognizing and dealing with problems

A large proportion of the feedback you receive will involve people raising problems that you will be expected to advise on or help solve. When this happens your first task will often be that of recognizing when the people you brief actually have a problem. This is not as easy as many business briefers imagine, even when you have monitored the people you brief informally (see Chapter 8) and believe that a problem may exist:

Exercise 8: Read the sequence below and answer the questions that follow. The briefer is advising his retail sales staff how to sell a satellite/TV set offer:

Briefer: 'All you have to say to a customer is: If you buy this TV set today and if you're thinking about buying a satellite system too, then, okay, you can have one. It'll only cost you £1!'
(Silence)
Briefer: 'Okay?'
Staff no 1: 'Mmm.'
Briefer: 'I've put a more detailed "how to do it" page in the sales technique book for you to read.'
Staff no 2: 'What about installation costs?'

Briefer: 'They have to pay for that, of course. Basically, they get the system for that price.'
Staff no 3: 'Won't it cost them £80 or £90 for installation?'
Briefer: 'No, no, no. If they take out an all-channel package it'll only cost 50 and that's not too bad.'
Staff no 1: 'Fifty pounds?'
Briefer: 'Yeah.'
Staff no 1: 'But it'll cost them even more if they don't take out a full package.'
Staff no 4: 'They'll never buy that.'
Staff no 5: 'Exactly!'
Briefer: 'They won't if you don't try, that's for sure.'
(Silence)
Briefer: 'Erm, has anybody got any other suggestions about how we can increase our business today?'

1. What problem do the sales staff have about this offer?
2. Where is the first possible sign that the sales staff have a problem?
3. When does the briefer explicitly deal with this problem?
4. How does the briefer solve this problem?

The answers are on page 76.

Most problems will become evident, at first, only in an implicit way. In this sense, the sequence above is typical. Indeed, problems tend to progress up a 'staircase' of explicitness and are usually only expressed explicitly or officially as a last resort:

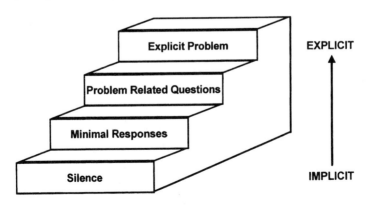

Figure 13 *The 'staircase' of explicitness*

- Silences are usually the first and most implicit sign that a problem exists (see line 4 in exercise 8). Silences like these usually last no longer than a second or so and are often followed by minimal responses (eg line 6).
- Minimal responses are often followed by proposal related questions (eg lines 9, 12 and 15).
- When these are ignored or passed over then the problem may be raised in a way that it difficult if not impossible for you to ignore.

The problem with silences and minimal responses is that, although they provide early indications that a problem exists, they do not usually provide you with sufficient information to figure out what that problem actually is. However, the sequence in exercise 8 is typical in one other way. Although the sales staff did not state their problem explicitly, they provided plenty of clues that were sufficient enough for their briefer to be able to figure out both that a problem existed and what that problem actually was.

When I started collecting recordings of real-life business briefings I was shocked at how many briefers tried to ignore an obvious but implicit problem. The briefer in exercise 8 was just one of many who did this. Even when a problem was explicit and was made difficult to ignore there were far too many occasions when a briefer did nothing more than dismiss that problem or deal with it (and maybe also the person who raised it) in an insensitive or unsympathetic way.

What could they have done instead? Firstly, whenever a problem is raised or hinted at it is almost always better to deal with it head-on and at the earliest possible opportunity. Figure 14 shows a 'best practice' problem-solving flow-chart. It will help you structure how you deal with and solve many of the problems raised during your own business briefings:

- It is vital that you start any problem solving discussion by checking that you (and everyone else present) understands what the problem actually is.
- When you explore both the nature and causes of the problem as well as the relative merits of adopting a particular solution it is important that you deal with the issue itself. Do not allow this discussion to get heated or personal.
- Do not be afraid to change your decision in the light of something someone else has said. Such behaviour is more likely to be perceived as a strength rather than a weakness.

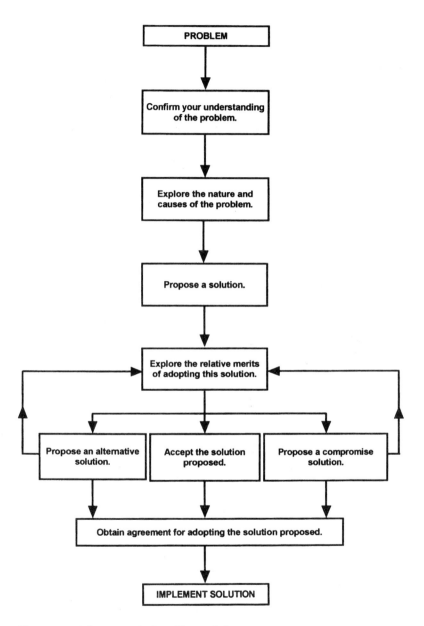

Figure 14 *A 'best practice' problem-solving sequence*

- At the end of a problem-solving discussion confirm verbally what has been decided (eg 'So, we're all agreed on X then?')
- Remember that it is not the absence of problems but how you deal with them when they arise that is a hallmark of an effective briefer.

Effective briefings need formal feedback. Feedback flourishes in briefings conducted within an atmosphere of consultation and consent rather than command and control and where the people being briefed feel confident that any contributions they make and any problems they raise are likely to be valued and acted on by you.

Exercise 7 page 68:
I found six main ways and nine ways in all:

1. The briefer appears not to have allowed enough time for any feedback.
2. He makes it obvious that there is no time for any feedback before he asks for it. First, by saying 'I've run over time'. Second, by pointing out that people are already waiting to enter the restaurant. Third, by asking his staff to open the restaurant doors for business.
3. The phrase 'Anything else?' is probably too curt and vague to encourage any specific and substantive feedback.
4. By not leaving any pauses before and after the word 'No?' he does not allow sufficient time for any of his staff to formulate any contribution they may have wished to make.
5. The word 'No?' in rapidly seeking confirmation that no one wants to speak also actively discourages anyone who may have been about to speak.
6. By expressing some pleasure at people not having any feedback (ie with the word 'Good') the briefer will surely only discourage people from contributing feedback on subsequent occasions.

How many of these did you recognize? The lower your score the more you will need to increase your sensitivity to the ways briefers can subtly but significantly deter people from providing valuable feedback.

Exercise 8 page 72:
1. The mandatory cost of installation – even the lowest priced option – will seriously deter people from purchasing the £1 satellite system.

2. The silence at line 4.
3. Lines 10–11.
4. He doesn't. He berates his staff for their poor attitude (line 20) and then gingerly moves on to another subject (lines 22–3).

CHAPTER 10
Routine

Most business briefings are given on a regular basis by the same briefer to the same group of people who, in turn, are repeatedly asked to accomplish the same kinds of objectives by performing the same kinds of tasks. Under these circumstances it is no wonder that, over time, the impact of such briefings tends to decline. Regular business briefers must take special steps to counteract this tendency otherwise their own performance and the performances of the people they brief will invariably suffer. This chapter outlines the tell-tale signs of briefing fatigue and shows you what steps you can take to keep your regular briefings fresh and effective.

Business briefings are fundamentally a pro-active communication tool. They should not be held only in emergencies; nor should they be held sporadically (eg 'if and when necessary'). They need to be held regularly to be most effective. But, as we can see in the table below, there are drawbacks as well as benefits in doing so.

BENEFITS	DRAWBACKS
The heightened familiarity between everyone present can lead to greater efficiency, effectiveness and team-spirit.	Familiarity can rapidly lead to overfamiliarity, particularly between briefer and briefed. This, in turn, can lead to boredom, complacency and an all-round decline in standards and performance.

BENEFITS	DRAWBACKS
Briefers can quickly develop a greater understanding of the abilities of the people they brief enabling them to appraise and nurture talent more successfully.	Rapidly exposes any deficiencies in a briefer's communication skills, particularly any lack of versatility.
Briefers can repeat and reinforce information given in previous briefings and thereby enhance the impact and understanding of what they say.	Repeated information can easily sound too repetitive, reducing dramatically the impact of what briefers say.
People are more likely to perform consistently and at a higher level if they are being informed, advised and encouraged on a regular basis.	Can be viewed as management interference, as if briefers do not have enough confidence in the people they brief to perform their tasks without constant and close supervision.
Briefers can provide information, advice and encouragement only when it is necessary and thus implement long term objectives on a step-by-step basis. Large amounts of complex information is more easily forgotten by people when it is delivered in a single briefing or when that information is not immediately relevant.	'Drip fed' information may prevent the people being briefed from seeing the big picture of a long term strategy, leading to feelings of alienation and accusations of lack of consultation and hidden agendas. Less than urgent objectives may be treated as being less than important objectives.
Feedback is more immediate, allowing problems to be raised and resolved more quickly.	Can encourage a culture of dependency where briefers are routinely expected to suggest solutions to all problems faced by the people being briefed.
Briefers have more opportunities to evaluate the effectiveness of their briefings, enabling them to rapidly improve the quality and impact of what they say.	Makes it more difficult for briefers to determine the precise impact and effectiveness of any individual briefing.

The main benefits and drawbacks of regular briefing

One task of every business briefer is to maximize the benefits and minimize the drawbacks created by regular briefing.

Recognizing briefing fatigue
The term 'briefing fatigue' refers to that situation where the quality and effectiveness of briefings as well as the subsequent performances of the people being briefed all decline as a result of the act of briefing people on a regular basis.

The four phases of regular briefing
When you hold regular briefings and do not attempt to minimize the drawbacks of doing so, your briefings will typically pass through four distinct stages of quality and effectiveness (see Figure 15):

- **New**. Effectiveness is relatively high and increases rapidly, not because of the quality of your skills as a briefer (which, at this stage, are likely to be low), but because the briefing process and the objectives, tasks and targets set within it, are novel for everyone concerned.
- **Maturing**. As your experience and skill grows and everyone becomes more familiar with the briefing process as well as each other, the quality and effectiveness of your briefings will continue steadily to increase. At least until you reach the highest possible point of effectiveness (point A in Figure 15).
- **Decline**. Over-familiarity triumphs over novelty and experience. Briefings and the objectives, tasks and targets set within them become routine; bad habits set in and effectiveness decreases progressively until the lowest point of effectiveness is reached (point B in Figure 15).
- **Wear-Out**. At this stage boredom and fatigue are commonplace for everyone. Briefings become markedly more repetitive. When this point is reached there is often little benefit to be obtained by continuing to hold briefings. Doing so may even make things much worse.

As a briefer, you should aim to reach and maintain point A, continually monitor for any signs of decline and try to avoid point B (and beyond) at all costs. Listed below are the main early warning signs of

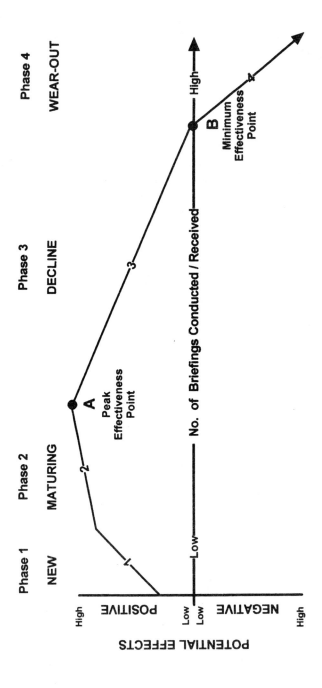

Figure 15 *The four phases of regular briefing*

briefing fatigue. Tick those changes you recognize in your own behaviour and in the behaviour of the people you brief. In each case, decide whether these changes are recent (ie have occurred only in your last three to five briefings) or are more well established:

Your own behaviour	Recent	Well Established
1. Your briefings start later or finish earlier than usual.	_____	_____
2. You cancel more briefings.	_____	_____
3. You spend less of your available time preparing your briefings.	_____	_____
4. The amount of practical advice contained in your briefing is noticeably lower than usual.	_____	_____
5. Your responses to suggestions, comments and questions are more critical and negative.	_____	_____
6. You repeat advice, instructions and encouragement more often.	_____	_____
7. You find yourself hoping that no one will prolong your briefing by providing any feedback or by asking questions.	_____	_____
8. You adopt a lecturing style of briefing rather than a more collaborative, consultative style.	_____	_____
9. When objectives are not reached or tasks remain unfinished you tend to blame the people you brief more than you blame yourself.	_____	_____
10. You are less pro-active – more problems are being postponed or ignored, rather than immediately addressed or successfully prevented.	_____	_____

The behaviour of the people you brief	Recent	Well Established
1. Non-attendance has increased.	_____	_____
2. Late arrivals are more common.	_____	_____
3. The amount of feedback you receive or the number of questions you are asked is lower than normal.	_____	_____
4. Standards and levels of performance of the people you brief have unexpectedly declined.	_____	_____
5. The people you brief seem less motivated to do what you ask.	_____	_____
6. Signs of boredom, restlessness or clock watching occur earlier in your briefing.	_____	_____
7. The people you brief are more critical and argumentative and nit-pick over seemingly unimportant things.	_____	_____
8. The quantity and quality of the feedback you receive is lower.	_____	_____
9. There is an increase in stifled expressions of impatience and disappointment when anyone makes a comment, asks a question etc, particularly towards the end of your briefings.	_____	_____
10. The people you brief have started to accept or agree with nearly everything you say, regardless of how controversial or problematic it may be.	_____	_____

What other problems have you noticed that may be the result of your regular briefing?

	Recent	Well Established
1. _____	_____	_____
2. _____	_____	_____
3. _____	_____	_____

The earlier you recognize these kinds of early warning signs the easier it will be for you to prevent or at least reduce briefing fatigue. The more early warning signs that exist and the more established they have become, the more urgent it is that you quickly do something about them.

Dealing with the common causes of briefing fatigue

Two of the most common underlying causes of briefing fatigue are over-briefing and a lack of versatility on the part of briefers. Knowing how to limit the negative effects of both will make it easier for you to maintain and maximize the benefits of regular briefing.

1. Over-briefing
If briefing fatigue is often partly the result of holding briefings more often than they need to be held then just how often *should* briefings be held? The answer to this question depends on two things: First, the frequency at which new information needs to be relayed/obtained. Second, the extent to which an obvious, performance-related benefit is obtained by relaying/obtaining this information in a briefing. In addition, other factors such as the availability of the people you brief, the difficulty of the objectives and tasks you set and how often you need to review work in progress will influence your decision. At the very least, business briefings should be held on a monthly basis.

This form of briefing fatigue can also be reduced by limiting the number of briefings delivered by any single briefer. Suitable alternatives for this course of action include:

- rotating the responsibility of giving briefings amongst your other managerial or supervisory colleagues;
- allowing high performing members of the people you brief to take the occasional (and, usually, a relatively less important) briefing;
- inviting your own manager/superior to take the occasional briefing. (They should not need to be asked.)

2. Lack of versatility
Versatile business briefers can call on a wide repertoire of communicative skills and strategies. They know which particular skills and strategies are most appropriate to use for the various situations and

circumstances that they and the people they brief are ever likely to face. And, more importantly, they regularly employ these skills and strategies. The process of regular briefing will almost certainly expose any lack of communicative and strategic versatility in a briefer.

Unnecessary repetition of information is, by far, the most common way a briefer's lack of versatility manifests itself. It also seems to be the major cause of briefing fatigue. The larger your vocabulary the more accurate and versatile you can be. Many briefers have difficulties selecting the most accurate word in the following three categories:

1. **Degrees of certainty**: eg, might, could, possibly, potentially, probably, likely, certainly, surely.
2. **Degrees of frequency**: eg, normally, generally, typically, mainly, predominantly, primarily, customarily, usually, commonly, always, sometimes, occasionally.
3. **Degrees of quantity**: eg, most, plenty, enough, a lot, several, largely, few, many, various, some.

Perhaps the best way of illustrating this problem is via assessments, ie the words you use when you evaluate or give an opinion or take a position on something or about someone.

Exercise 9: Write down as many assessments as you can in the appropriate columns in the table below. I have given you an example of each of the five different strengths of assessments (ranging from very negative to very positive) to start you off. Compare your answers with mine on page 87.

VERY NEGATIVE (–)	NEGATIVE (-)	NEUTRAL (+/-)	POSITIVE (+)	VERY POSITIVE (+ +)
Appalling.	Annoying.	Acceptable.	Admirable.	Awesome.

How to Give Effective Business Briefings

VERY NEGATIVE (–)	NEGATIVE (-)	NEUTRAL (+/-)	POSITIVE (+)	VERY POSITIVE (+ +)

Listed below are a series of measures you can take to reduce unnecessary repetition and improve your versatility and effectiveness:

- Try to use the widest possible range of different (but equally effective) ways of saying those things you cannot avoid repeating.
- Be more accurate, specific and detailed for each point you make.
- Use different kinds of examples, evidence and statistics.
- Try to find ways of saying things in unusual and novel ways.
- Vary the beginnings and endings of your briefings.
- Vary the format and style of your briefings.
- Use high impact oratory to increase impact and memorability.
- Improve the quality and relevance of any practical advice you give.

If you find that a significant proportion of your briefings are dealing with previously stated information and advice etc. then check to ensure that it has been understood and whether it is being acted on or ignored. If you find that the information you receive from higher management to relay to others is a major reason for your repetition then encourage higher management to take more responsibility for the repetitive briefs they send. For example, you could ask them to include advice (and even a sample script) showing how the information could be relayed to the people you brief in the most effective way.

It is worth remembering that many of the problems generated as a result of briefing people regularly are the result of preventable communicative and performance deficiencies of the briefers themselves, even when these problems appear to stem from your managers and/ or the people being briefed. As such, many of these problems can be reduced, if not prevented altogether, by preparing your briefings properly and briefing people effectively.

Read through your responses to the 'signs of briefing fatigue checklist' earlier in this chapter. Rate each of those you ticked, from 1–10, in terms of their relative severity. (1 = low; 10 = high.)

1: List the three worst problems you are experiencing as a result of regular briefing:

i: _____

ii: _____

iii: _____

2: What do you think are the reasons for these problems?

i: _____

ii: _____

iii: _____

3: How do you propose to solve these problems?

i: _____

ii: _____

iii: _____

Exercise 9 page 85:
Here are just a few of the assessments you could have selected.

VERY NEGATIVE (–)	NEGATIVE (-)	NEUTRAL (+/-)	POSITIVE (+)	VERY POSITIVE (++)
Appalling	Adrift	Acceptable	Admirable	Amazing
Awful	Annoying	Adequate	Beneficial	Astonishing
Dire	Apathetic	Agreeable	Better	Awesome
Disastrous	Bad	All right	Commendable	Beautiful
Disgraceful	Crappy	Ample	Constructive	Brilliant
Disgusting	Deficient	Appropriate	Delightful	Excellent
Dreadful	Disappointing	Average	Encouraging	Exceptional
Garbage	Embarrassing	Decent	Favourable	Extraordinary
Ghastly	Feeble	Enough	Good	Fabulous
Gross	Frustrating	Fair	Helpful	Fantastic
Hideous	Irritating	Feasible	Impressive	Great

How to Give Effective Business Briefings

Horrible	Lacking	Fine	Lovely	Incredible
Horrific	Lagging	Moderate	Nice	Magnificent
Inadequate	Low	Neat	Pleasant	Marvellous
Intolerable	Negative	Normal	Pleasing	Outstanding
Mediocre	Poor	Not bad	Positive	Phenomenal
Monstrous	Rotten	Okay	Pretty	Remarkable
Outrageous	Second-rate	Passable	Productive	Sensational
Pathetic	Struggling	Reasonable	Promising	Spectacular
Rubbish	Sub-standard	Satisfactory	Rewarding	Splendid
Severe	Unacceptable	Sound	Superior	Superb
Shocking	Unimpressive	Sufficient	Useful	Terrific
Stupid	Unpleasant	Suitable	Valuable	Tremendous
Terrible	Unsatisfactory	Tolerable	Well	Unbeatable
Ugly	Wanting	Useable	Worthwhile	Unbelievable
Wretched	Weak	Usual	Worthy	Wonderful

CHAPTER 11
Variations

This book has concentrated on the skills required for relaying information to and/or obtaining information from relatively small and well-established groups of people by an immediate and familiar superior. You will find, however, that the vast majority of these skills can be applied to any kind of briefing situation. This chapter focuses on the other kinds of business briefing situations you are most likely to encounter and outlines a variety of additional skills you will need to employ to deliver them effectively.

Crisis briefings

In these briefings some form of information must be relayed or obtained or some form of problem solved or action taken with the utmost of urgency. Rumours from the grapevine will ensure that tension is high among the people you brief and you will have to maintain full control of your briefing to ensure that everyone stays focused on the issue at hand. Indeed, this is probably the only kind of briefing situation where it is often advantageous to adopt a more autocratic briefing style.

- Your briefing must be solution orientated. Concentrate on relaying or obtaining only the essential 'What?', 'Where?', 'How?' and 'When?' types of information rather than the 'Why?'.
- Outline the nature of the crisis in your introduction. Detail what you expect from every person present and explain how their individual efforts will play a vital role in helping overcome the crisis.
- Try to minimize the need for any non-essential participation and feedback. If you do adopt a more autocratic style you should stress

that it is only going to be a temporary, short-term measure. When the crisis is over make sure that this style *was* only temporary.

- You will probably not have enough time to employ any elaborate motivational strategies but if the people you brief are professional and committed, then the crisis alone should be sufficient enough to motivate them.

- Emphasize any benefits that will accrue to your organization and, even better, to the people you brief when they help overcome the crisis in question.

- Stay calm while delivering your briefing. Any signs of panic or tension will invariably be noticed by and transferred to the people you brief.

- The people you brief will almost certainly want to know what *you* are planning to do to help overcome the crisis. Tell them. A crisis is the best possible time to lead from the front by means of personal and practical example.

- If you have the time, distribute notes confirming what you have said to reduce any misunderstandings about actions needed and everyone's individual tasks and responsibilities.

- Save any detailed discussion of who or what is responsible for the crisis and how such a crisis can be prevented from happening again until *after* the crisis is over.

Do not be tempted to turn every briefing into a crisis briefing in order to save time, reduce audience participation or dodge the prospect of receiving negative feedback. Crisis briefings should be saved for genuine emergencies only.

Multi-briefer briefings

When two or more briefers deliver a briefing together, effectiveness depends primarily on how successfully that briefing is prepared and co-ordinated.

Appoint one briefer to take overall responsibility for co-ordinating the briefing. This person should be in charge of:

- preparing and delivering the introduction and summary;
- announcing who each briefer is and what they are going to say;
- collating any handouts or confirming notes to be distributed as a single package;

- presenting any overheads and slides, etc;
- managing the feedback during the briefing;
- and, more generally, ensuring that individual briefers do not talk longer than agreed or unnecessarily repeat what other briefers have said.

Decide on and stick rigidly to a maximum time limit for each briefer's contribution. To improve understanding, ensure that the order in which each briefer speaks is based either on a logical or chronological sequence or on the relative importance of the information they will be presenting.

It may be necessary before the briefing to agree to take a unified strategy for dealing with any problems you anticipate will be raised in feedback. Any disagreement between briefers is liable to be treated as a sign of weakness in your arguments or proposals.

The number of briefers (and, thus, the number of changeovers between speakers) should, whenever possible, be kept to a minimum to avoid disturbing the flow of the briefing. Ideally, each briefer (apart from the briefing co-ordinator) should only have one presentational slot.

Briefing superiors

This is one of the rare situations where any final decision about a course of action to be taken is most likely to be made by the people being briefed brief rather than by you the briefer. Accordingly, your emphasis will need to be on the accuracy, relevance and objectivity of the information you present and on making the best use of the time you have been allocated.

- Don't allow yourself to be rushed. Pre-agree a time limit for your briefing and reiterate this agreement in your introduction.
- Expect interruptions and criticisms. Try to encourage your superiors to ask questions and provide feedback *after* you have completed your briefing.
- Stick to the essentials. Your superiors will deem their time to be more valuable than yours.
- Telegraph where all your major points are leading to.
- Give hard evidence to justify all your major points and recommendations.

- While you will not be expected to use your briefing to motivate your superiors they will probably need to know the level of motivation of the people who will be carrying out any tasks related to the subject matter of your briefing.

Duplicate briefing

In this briefing situation you have to deliver the same briefing to different groups of people. Typically, these groups will be working on similar tasks and/or towards the same objective but cannot all be briefed at the same time or venue. The main problem you will have to guard against here is the complacency that can emerge as a result of your increased familiarity with the information you are presenting. This can lead to vitally important information remaining unsaid.

- Aim for consistency in terms of the planned content of your briefings. Write down what you need to say and, as a minimum, always say *everything* you have written down.
- Always remember that what becomes progressively more familiar to you is unlikely to be at all familiar to the people you brief.
- Keep each group posted as to what other groups are doing. Any feedback you receive from one group is probably going to be relevant to other groups. So be prepared to alter the content of your subsequent briefings and to distribute update or feedback memos to any groups you already have briefed.

Giving an impromptu briefing

There are two problems commonly faced by people who have to deliver a briefing without advance notice. First, compensating for having insufficient time to properly prepare what needs to be said; and, second, having to talk without the help of detailed, if any, notes. Both problems can be significantly reduced by employing the following highly compressed version of the advice contained in Chapters 3 and 4 of this book.

- Limit your briefing to one major, clear and specific objective. This should be the very first thing you say.
- Deliver your briefing within a simple, three-part structure, ie your introduction (what you are going to say), the substance of your

brief (where you say what you need to say) and your summary (where you reiterate what you have just said).

- Structure each topic by adopting the following three-step method: i) Detail the 'What?', 'How?', 'Where?', 'When' and 'Why?' elements of that topic; ii) Describe any potentially negative internal/external factors; iii) Provide the required explanations and advice.
- Speak slower and leave longer silences between your sentences to give yourself more time to think about what you are going to say next.
- If any of the information you need to relay is written down (eg in a fax or memo), provide a copy to each person present as confirming notes.
- Encourage people to ask questions and provide feedback after you have completed your briefing.

Briefing strangers

When you brief people who are unfamiliar to you or unfamiliar with one another you will almost certainly have to deal with the problems of nervousness and anxiety – not just your own but also amongst the people you brief.

- If you feel very nervous, speak more slowly and in a louder voice. The former will help keep you calm, the latter will at least make you sound more confident.
- If you are a stranger, the people you brief are more likely to be nervous of you, so you should not expect lots of participation or high quality feedback without providing plenty of positive encouragement. Trust takes time.
- Start the session by getting each person present to say who they are and what they do. Ask them also to quickly brief you about their experiences and opinions of the topic at hand. This will help break the ice and will compensate for your own (and anyone else's) lack of familiarity with the people you are briefing.
- Make a quick note of what they say and where they are sitting or standing. Whenever you ask for feedback from anyone you can then confidently refer to that person by their name and their position (eg 'Thomas, as senior buyer . . .') and thereby refresh everyone else's memory.

Briefing large groups

The problems you will face whenever you have to brief a group of, say, thirty or more people will mainly have to do with ensuring your information is heard and seen. You may also have to encourage people to overcome their natural reluctance to participate when so many other people are present.

- Make the content of all overheads and slides as simple as possible. Use extra large format text and bold, highly simplified visuals. Better still, distribute handouts.
- Place any handouts at the ends of each row of seating before your briefing begins. This will help reduce the disruption that occurs when they have to be distributed.
- In large areas (auditoriums, lecture halls, etc) try to get everyone to sit together and as close to you as possible. As people enter the room instruct them to fill the available seating centrally and from front to back. People who are closer together are easier to manage.
- Refrain from using a microphone unless it is absolutely necessary. The added amplitude often encourages people to start talking among themselves. Instead, speak in a louder voice but without resorting to shouting.
- To stimulate questions and feedback start by asking particular people to answer *specific* questions, eg 'Anna, as site manager, what do you think the consequences of what I have said will be?' React positively and supportively, then ask for comments from your audience at large. Be prepared to wait longer than usual before receiving any response.
- Do not forget the importance of continually establishing brief and friendly eye contact with everyone present; however far away they are from you it will still be noticed and appreciated.

Decision briefings

Your main problem here is likely to be that of deciding on how many different possible options or courses of action should be relayed to or obtained from the people you brief before a final decision can confidently be taken. Many business briefers find it best to select at least three, the two most obvious and opposing alternatives and a third, middle or compromise option. Regardless of how many options you decide to deliver or obtain it is also good practice to indicate which of these options you consider to be the best and why. The credibility of the particular course of action you suggest will be severely undermined unless you have described or discussed the advantages and disadvantages of each option raised in an objective and well-balanced way.

CHAPTER 12
Evaluation

Regularly evaluating your business briefings will help you discover the impact of what you have said (and how you have said it) on the people you brief. More importantly, it will also help you to determine what needs to be done to make your briefings more effective. This chapter describes the type of evaluations you can conduct and how best to use the information you obtain.

Evaluating the performance outcome

The acid test of your briefing ability should be the subsequent performance of the people you have briefed. The most obvious way to measure this is by finding out, at the appropriate time, whether your objective (and each particular task or target you specified) was achieved. For example, if your objective was to increase sales of product X by 15 per cent over the next 3 months, then all you need to do is compare this objective with the actual sales of product X after those three months have elapsed.

But achieving your objective does not necessarily mean your briefing was effective. You will need to discover *how* your objective was achieved and, if it was not, then *why* not. One of the best ways of doing this is via a debriefing session.

Debriefings
This is a post-mortem meeting with the people you have briefed where issues related to the objectives set and tasks specified in your previous briefing are discussed. These are the types of issues you would review.

- Was the time period assigned for particular tasks to be completed reasonable?
- Did the people you briefed actually employ the information and advice you gave them?
- To what extent was the information and advice you provided responsible for the outcome generated?
- Did any unforeseen factors (both internal and external) positively or negatively affect the performance of the people you briefed?
- Had the people you briefed received sufficient support, training and resources to complete their tasks?
- Was the person you allocated a particular task to the most suitable person for that task?

The character of these meetings should be akin to a no-holds-barred brainstorming session where everyone is expected to candidly contribute their own particular opinions and experiences. Of course, in order to maximise their benefit, debriefings should only be held after the time period allocated for the particular tasks and objectives under discussion has elapsed. Instead of holding a special meeting for this purpose, it will usually be more convenient for everyone concerned to incorporate each debriefing into the next business briefing you hold with the same group of participants.

Evaluating the presentational impact

To fully appreciate the impact your briefings have on the people you brief you will also need to evaluate the quality of the content, delivery and general style of your briefings. You can do this either by some form of self-evaluation or by asking or testing the people you have briefed.

Self-evaluation
Find somewhere you won't be disturbed and try to relive your briefing moment-by-moment, word-by-word and gesture-by-gesture. The most important things to review are your listeners' verbal and non-verbal reactions to:

- each objective, task or target you announced;
- information, advice and explanations you gave;
- any specific communication technique you used;
- your own reactions and responses to questions, comments, suggestions, disagreements etc from the people at your briefing.

Make notes of anything you feel needs improving. The success of your self-evaluation will ultimately depend on two things:

1. Your ability to determine what particular verbal or non-verbal behaviour has generated which particular reactions and responses during your briefing.
2. Your ability to interpret what those reactions and responses actually mean.

The forms on pages 99 and 100 will help you self-evaluate both the performance outcome and the presentational impact of your briefings:

Evaluating the people you brief

Briefers are rarely the best judges of the quality and impact of what they say. For this reason alone, it is important that you consult the people you brief when undertaking an evaluation of your presentational style. Indeed, what briefers think and what the people they brief think about a briefing are often two entirely different things. The former tend, in particular, to overestimate the quality and influence of their briefings, especially the quality and the influence of their advice and their motivational strategies. They also have a tendency to attribute any problems in the delivery of their briefings to *organizational* factors (eg not having a white-board to present key points, not having had enough preparation time).

In contrast, recipients of briefings are much more likely to attribute any problems in the delivery of those briefings to *communicative* problems on the part of the briefer (eg lack of information, advice, clarity; too much repetition, etc).

But what type of impact evaluations should you conduct? Put simply, if you want to know people's attitudes and opinions of your briefing style you should use post-briefing questionnaires. Alternatively, if you want to discover what people remember about the content or structure of your briefing you should conduct post-briefing tests.

Post-briefing questionnaires

You could start this type of evaluation by giving copies of the Performance Outcome and Presentational Impact forms to the people at your briefings and compare their responses with your own. Other questionnaires that you devise would probably include the following kinds of questions:

Performance Outcome Form

Date:___ / ___ / ___Briefing: _____
Objective, task or target: _____
_____
_____
_____

1: *ATTAINABILITY* of objective, task or target:
(Easy) – 0 1 2 3 4 Average 6 7 8 9 10 – (Hard)
Improvements needed: _____
_____
_____
_____

2: *QUALITY* of support, training and resources etc.:
(Low) – 0 1 2 3 4 Average 6 7 8 9 10 – (High)
Improvements needed: _____
_____
_____
_____

3: *USE* of information and advice provided:
(Low) – 0 1 2 3 4 Average 6 7 8 9 10 – (High)
Improvements needed: _____
_____
_____

4: *INFLUENCE* of briefing on subsequent behaviour:
(Low) – 0 1 2 3 4 Average 6 7 8 9 10 – (High)
Improvements needed: _____
_____
_____
_____

Comments: _____
_____
_____

Presentational Impact Form

Date:___ / ___ / ___Briefing:_____

BRIEFER
Preparation and Structure:
(Low) – 0 1 2 3 4 Average 6 7 8 9 10 – (High)

Communication Style: (clarity, understandability, accuracy, etc)
(Low) – 0 1 2 3 4 Average 6 7 8 9 10 – (High)

Factual Speech: (info / advice on objectives, tasks, targets, etc)
(Low) – 0 1 2 3 4 Average 6 7 8 9 10 – (High)

Emotive Speech: (words of motivation, encouragement, etc)
(Low) – 0 1 2 3 4 Average 6 7 8 9 10 – (High)

Responsiveness to Feedback:
(Low) – 0 1 2 3 4 Average 6 7 8 9 10 – (High)

Comments/Improvements needed: _____
_____
_____
_____

BRIEFED
Attentiveness and Interest:
(Low) – 0 1 2 3 4 Average 6 7 8 9 10 – (High)

Motivation, enthusiasm and team-spirit:
(Low) – 0 1 2 3 4 Average 6 7 8 9 10 – (High)

Feedback (comments, suggestions, questions, etc):
(Low) – 0 1 2 3 4 Average 6 7 8 9 10 – (High)

Comments/Improvements needed: _____
_____

- How could this briefing have been delivered more effectively?
- Did you find the particular technique/advice/information I gave useful?
- What, in your opinion, was the most important point mentioned in the briefing you have just received?

- What, in your opinion, were the three best and worst parts of this briefing?
- Were there any parts of this briefing you did not understand?
- How would you compare the level of information/advice/motivation contained in this briefing with that which would be contained in an ideal briefing? (Get people to provide relative percentages for their answers to this type of question.)

Leave plenty of space below each question and encourage people to provide long and detailed responses, as well as reasons why they have provided a particular answer. You could also incorporate rating scales (like those contained in the two forms above) into your questionnaires. They will make it easier for you to quantify any similarities and differences between people's responses. But if you do use rating scales, discourage people from persistently answering 'average' as a response.

In your analysis of these responses you should pay close attention to any major discrepancies between:

- an individual's evaluation ratings for different questions;
- the responses given by different briefing recipients for any particular question;
- the most common response of the people you brief and your own response to any particular question; and
- the responses people give for different briefings you evaluate.

Post-briefing tests
This is an excellent way to evaluate people's level of recall and understanding of your briefing in general or of any specific instructions, advice or objectives within it. Simply give everyone present a blank sheet of paper and ask them questions such as:

- List, in order of importance, all the key points you remember from the briefing you have just received.
- What were the X number of steps I said you needed to take to successfully complete the Y procedure?
- Which techniques did I recommend you to use to accomplish X?

Generally, the greater the similarity between what you said in your briefing and what the people you have briefed have written down the better your briefing has been communicated.

Conduct these questionnaires and tests without giving the people you brief any prior warning. Their responses will not then be biased as a result of them having listened to your briefing any differently.

The time at which you conduct these evaluations, what you ask and how you ask it will all influence the type of information you will obtain, particularly in terms of the accuracy of that information. The two main options available to you are *before* work on the tasks related to your objectives has been started and *after* the objectives, tasks or targets have been attempted, completed or achieved.

Questionnaires conducted immediately after your briefing tend to receive higher than usual ratings, especially if people expect to complete/achieve their set tasks. Any test you conduct at this point is likely to have the highest level of accurate recall. Questionnaires given after tasks have been attempted are more likely to contain critical remarks about the nature of the information and advice you gave, especially if people have failed to accomplish their tasks or targets or your objectives were not achieved.

By using the same type of evaluation after different briefings you will be able to compare how people's perceptions of your performance has improved or declined over time. If you use a combination of evaluation methods at any one time you will obtain not only a more comprehensive but also a more accurate appraisal of the quality of your briefing skill. In the research I have conducted into real-life business briefings I obtained many examples of recipients of briefings claiming (in post-briefing questionnaires) that the briefing they received could *not* have been delivered more effectively. However, when they were asked (in post-briefing tests) to recall important information from the briefing they received many were unable to do so.

Using evaluations

The amount of information you can obtain from even the most basic evaluations you conduct can easily become overwhelming and, therefore, you will often have to decide which particular aspect of your briefing style requires the most immediate improvement. Concentrate on improving only one or two areas or communication skills per briefing. Keep referring back to previous briefings to ensure that you are still using any new skills that you have adopted.

Always be prepared to quickly abandon a newly introduced technique if it does not appear to be working. Above all, make sure that the people you brief can see that you are using the evaluation information they have provided to improve the quality and style of your briefings.

Do not use any of the information you receive as ammunition against the people you brief, especially when it is critical of your own abilities and performance. It will almost certainly alienate them and seriously reduce the quality and accuracy of their responses in any subsequent evaluations you conduct. The best policy is to conduct all evaluations anonymously and to treat the information you receive from them as confidential.

Briefing? It's like sex, isn't it? We always think we're brilliant at it but most of us are far too afraid to ask for anyone else's opinion, just in case we discover that we're not.
Industrial supplies manager (Male)

Many briefers have an aversion to judging the effectiveness of their briefings solely in terms of improved performance of the people they brief. They argue that not all objectives are quantifiable – that, for example, someone may not have completed a particular task but other important factors such as their level of skill or motivation may have improved as a result of the briefing they received. Of course, it *is* difficult to accurately quantify the effectiveness of briefings (or any particular technique employed within them). Nobody is immune from the influence of negative internal and external factors (such as a lack of resources, customer reluctance to buy, etc). Factors like these may mean the objectives set in a briefing are not accomplished even though the quality and impact of the briefing itself was very high.

However, at the other extreme, judging effectiveness solely in terms of presentational impact can be a sign that you are treating the briefing process as an end in itself rather than the means to an end that it almost always should be. The main thing is that *some* form of evaluation should be conducted and that the evaluation you conduct, *whenever possible*, should include a quantifiable, objective related component. At the very least the process of evaluation, when undertaken on a regular basis, will undoubtedly reinforce positively the consultative, problem-solving, improvement orientated culture that is an essential ingredient for effective business briefing.

References

Bull, R C H (1979) A further study of improving the effectiveness of daily briefings, *Police Research Bulletin*, vol. 33 pp 18–22

Clark, C (1997) *The Communication and Motivations Skills Employed by Retail Store Managers During Morning Briefings*, Research Report

The Industrial Society (May 1994) 'Managing Best Practice (Report no. 1) Employee Communications', The Industrial Society, London

Ogilvy, D (1995) *Ogilvy on Advertising*, Prion, London